Cambridge Certificate of Proficiency in English 2

TEACHER'S BOOK

Examination papers from the University of Cambridge Local Examinations Syndicate

CAMBRIDGE
UNIVERSITY PRESS

PUBLISHED BY THE PRESS SYNDICATE OF THE UNIVERSITY OF CAMBRIDGE
The Pitt Building, Trumpington Street, Cambridge, United Kingdom

CAMBRIDGE UNIVERSITY PRESS
The Edinburgh Building, Cambridge CB2 2RU, UK
40 West 20th Street, New York NY 10011–4211, USA
477 Williamstown Road, Port Melbourne, VIC 3207, Australia
Ruiz de Alarcón 13, 28014 Madrid, Spain
Dock House, The Waterfront, Cape Town 8001, South Africa

http://www.cambridge.org

First published 2002

Printed in the United Kingdom at the University Press, Cambridge

ISBN 0 521 01168 X Student's Book
ISBN 0 521 75109 8 Student's Book with answers
ISBN 0 521 75104 7 Self-study Pack
ISBN 0 521 75107 1 Teacher's Book
ISBN 0 521 75106 3 Set of 2 Cassettes
ISBN 0 521 75105 5 Set of 2 Audio CDs

Contents

Introduction

The level of CPE

UCLES (University of Cambridge Local Examinations Syndicate) has developed a series of examinations with similar characteristics spanning five levels. Within the series of five levels, the Certificate of Proficiency in English (CPE) is at Cambridge Level 5.

Cambridge Level 5 Certificate of Proficiency in English (CPE)
Cambridge Level 4 Certificate in Advanced English (CAE)
Cambridge Level 3 First Certificate in English (FCE)
Cambridge Level 2 Preliminary English Test (PET)
Cambridge Level 1 Key English Test (KET)

CPE offers a high-level qualification for those wishing to use English for professional or study purposes. CPE is recognised by the majority of British universities for English language entrance requirements. It is suitable in content for candidates who have achieved a certain degree of maturity in their handling of abstract ideas and concepts. At this level the learner is approaching the linguistic competence of an educated native speaker.

The revision of CPE

Regular updating has allowed CPE to keep pace with changes in language teaching and testing. From December 2002, candidates will be taking the revised format of the examination.

CPE candidates

In 2000 there were approximately 50,000 candidates for CPE throughout the world. The candidates come from a wide range of backgrounds and take the examination for a number of different reasons. The following points summarise the characteristics of the current CPE candidature.

Nationality

CPE is taken by candidates in about 90 countries. The majority of these candidates enter for CPE in European or South American countries. Many candidates take CPE in the UK.

Age and gender

Most CPE candidates are in their late teenage years or early 20s. Almost 75% of all candidates are 25 years of age or under. Only around 5% of the candidature is 31 years of age or over. Approximately 70% of the total candidate population is female.

Employment

Most candidates are students, although the proportion varies significantly from country to country.

Preparation

Around 85% of all candidates undertake preparatory courses before the exam. Many candidates have taken other Cambridge examinations before. The most popular is FCE followed by CAE.

Reasons for taking CPE

The most frequent reason for candidates wanting an English language qualification is for work in their own country. Other reasons include work in another country and further study.

Further information

CPE is held each year in June and December in more than 850 centres worldwide. Special arrangements are available for disabled candidates. These may include extra time, separate accommodation or equipment, Braille transcription, etc. Consult the UCLES Local Secretary in your area for more details.

Copies of the regulations and details of entry procedure, current fees and further information about this and other Cambridge examinations can be obtained from the Local Secretary for UCLES examinations in your area or from:

EFL Information
University of Cambridge Local Examinations Syndicate
1 Hills Road
Cambridge
CB1 2EU
United Kingdom

Tel: +44 1223 553355
Fax: +44 1223 460278
e-mail: efl@ucles.org.uk
www.cambridge-efl.org.uk

In some areas, this information can also be obtained from the British Council.

CPE content and marking

The structure of CPE: *an overview*

The CPE examination consists of five papers:

Paper 1	Reading	1 hour 30 minutes
Paper 2	Writing	2 hours
Paper 3	Use of English	1 hour 30 minutes
Paper 4	Listening	40 minutes (approximately)
Paper 5	Speaking	19 minutes

Material used throughout CPE is as far as possible authentic and free of bias, and reflects the international flavour of the examination. The subject matter should not advantage or disadvantage certain groups of candidates, nor should it offend in areas such as religion, politics or sex.

Paper 1   Reading

The CPE Reading paper consists of four parts and 40 questions. The time allowed to select answers and record them on the answer sheet is one hour and thirty minutes.

Texts

The length of CPE texts varies from 130 words to 1100 words, depending on the task. The total length of texts over all four parts is approximately 3000 words. The texts cover a range of recently published material and appear in authentic form, presentation and content.
   Texts may be of the following types:
* informational
* opinion/comment
* discursive
* descriptive
* advice/instructional
* narrative
* imaginative/journalistic
* persuasive
* complaint
* combined, e.g. narrative/descriptive, information/opinion

Materials from fiction, non-fiction, journals, magazines, newspapers and promotional and informational material may be included.

Reading texts may contain some lexis unknown to candidates and understanding of these words may be tested if it can reasonably be expected that the meaning can be deduced from context (one of the skills tested in the paper).

Test focus

The tasks in the Reading paper test candidates' ability to:

- understand lexical appropriacy
- understand the gist of a text and its overall function and message
- interpret the text for inference, attitude and style
- select the relevant information from the text required to perform a task
- infer underlying meaning
- demonstrate an understanding of how text structure operates

Paper 1 outline

Part	Task type and focus	Number of questions	Task format
1	Four-option multiple-choice lexical cloze Idioms, collocations, fixed phrases, complementation, phrasal verbs, semantic precision	18	Three modified cloze texts, from a range of sources. Each text contains six gaps and is followed by six four-option multiple-choice questions.
2	Four-option multiple choice Content/detail, opinion, attitude, tone, purpose, main idea, implication, text organisation features (exemplification, comparison, reference)	8	Four texts on one theme, from a range of sources. Two four-option multiple-choice questions per text.
3	Gapped text Cohension, coherence, text structure, global meaning	7	One text from which paragraphs have been removed and placed in jumbled order after the text. Candidates must decide from where in the text the paragraphs have been removed.
4	Four-option multiple choice Focus as for Part 2	7	One text with seven four-option multiple-choice questions.

Marks

Candidates record their answers in pencil on a separate answer sheet. One mark is given for each correct answer in Part 1; two marks are given for each correct answer in Parts 2–4. The total score is then weighted to 40 marks for the whole Reading paper.

Marking

The Reading paper answer sheet is directly scanned by computer.

Paper 2 Writing

The CPE Writing paper requires candidates to answer two questions. Candidates are asked to write between 300 and 350 words for each answer. The time allowed is two hours.

Test focus

All questions specify the role of the reader, the role of the writer and the purpose for writing. Candidates are expected to show that they are sensitive to the kind of writing required to fulfil a task.

Part 1 tests candidates' ability to complete a task with a discursive focus. For example, candidates may be required to defend or attack a particular argument or opinion, compare or contrast an argument, explain a problem and suggest a solution or make recommendations having evaluated an idea.

In Part 2, candidates may be required to demonstrate a range of skills including narrating, analysing, hypothesising, describing, giving reasons, persuading and judging priorities.

Tasks

In both sections candidates are asked to complete non-specialist tasks with a range of formats. Presentation, register and style should be appropriate to the task and the effect on the target reader should always be borne in mind by the candidate.

In Part 1 candidates are asked to produce one piece of writing (300–350 words) in response to instructions and a short text. The language of the text is well within the level expected of CPE candidates and may come from a variety of sources, for example, extracts from newspapers, magazines, books, letters or advertisements. Visuals, such as a diagram, simple graph or picture, may be included with the text to support or extend a topic. In order to complete the tasks successfully, candidates need to use the text provided in an appropriate way by, as it states in the instructions, discussing the points raised and expressing their own opinions. They should avoid simply reproducing the text in their answers.

In Part 2, candidates have a choice of tasks within a variety of formats. Each task is contextualised by instructions of no more than 70 words. One of the optional tasks (question 5) is on background reading texts. There are three alternatives in question 5 and candidates may select one of these based on their reading of the set texts. The list of set texts is published by UCLES in the Examination Regulations. Each text normally remains on the list for two years.

Paper 2 outline

Part	Task type and focus	Number of tasks and length	Task format
1	Candidates are expected to write within the following formats: • an article • an essay • a letter • a proposal Discursive – presenting and developing arguments, expressing and supporting opinions, evaluating ideas, etc.	One compulsory task 300–350 words	A contextualised writing task giving candidates guidance to the context through instructions and one short text which may be supported by visual prompts.
2	Candidates are expected to write within the following formats for questions 2 to 4: • an article • a letter • a proposal • a review • a report Candidates are expected to write within the following formats for question 5: • an article • an essay • a letter • a review • a report Describing, persuading, narrating, evaluating, making recommendations, giving information, summarising, etc.	Four questions from which candidates choose one. One of the choices includes a question on each of the three set texts. 300–350 words	A contextualised writing task specified in no more than 70 words.

Assessment

An impression mark is awarded to each piece of writing using the general mark scheme. Examiners use band descriptors to assess language and task achievement. Each piece of writing is assigned to a band between 0 and 5 and can be awarded one of three performance levels within that band. For example, in Band 4, 4.1 represents weaker performance within Band 4; 4.2 represents typical performance within Band 4; 4.3 represents strong performance within Band 4. Acceptable performance at CPE level is represented by a band of 3. All tasks carry the same maximum mark.

The general impression mark scheme is used in conjunction with a task-specific mark scheme, which focuses on content, range of structures, vocabulary, organisation, register and format and the effect on the target reader of a specific task.

American spelling and usage is acceptable.

Band 5	Outstanding realisation of the task set shown by: • use of an extensive range of vocabulary, structures and expression • register and format wholly appropriate to the task set • skilful organisation with excellent development of the topic • minimal error Overall: impresses the reader and has a very positive effect
Band 4	Good realisation of the task set shown by: • use of a range of vocabulary, structures and expression • register and format appropriate to the task set • good organisation and development of the topic • minor errors Overall: has a positive effect on the reader
Band 3	Satisfactory realisation of the task set shown by: • use of an adequate range of vocabulary, structures and expression • register and format generally appropriate to the task set • generally clear organisation with adequate coverage of the topic • some non-impeding errors Overall: achieves the desired effect on the reader
Band 2	Inadequate attempt at the task set shown by: • limited range and/or inaccurate use of vocabulary, structures and expression • some attempt at appropriate register and format for the task set • some attempt at organisation, but lack of coherence – inadequate development of the topic • a number of errors, which sometimes impede communication Overall: has a negative effect on the reader
Band 1	Poor attempt at the task set shown by: • severely limited range and inaccurate use of vocabulary, structures and expression • little or no attempt at register and format for the task set • poor organisation, leading to incoherence – little relevance to the topic, and/or insufficient length • numerous errors, which distract and often impede communication Overall: has a very negative effect on the reader
Band 0	Negligible or no attempt at the task set: • incomprehensible due to serious error • totally irrelevant • insufficient language to assess • totally illegible

Marking

The panel of examiners is divided into small teams, each with a very experienced examiner as Team Leader. The Principal Examiner guides and monitors the marking process, which begins with a meeting of the Principal Examiner and the Team Leaders. This is held immediately after the examination and establishes a common standard of assessment by the selection of sample scripts for all five questions in Paper 2. These are chosen to demonstrate the range of responses and different levels of competence, and a task-specific mark scheme is finalised for each individual question on the paper. This summarises the content, organisation, range of structures and vocabulary, register and format which would be found in a satisfactory response to the question. The overall effect on the target reader is also specified. The accuracy of language, including spelling and punctuation, is assessed on the general impression scale for all tasks. Examiners refer to these mark schemes as they mark each script. A rigorous process of co-ordination and checking is carried out before and throughout the marking process.

Paper 3 Use of English

The CPE Use of English paper consists of five parts and 44 questions. The time allowed for completing all five parts and recording answers on the answer sheets is one hour and thirty minutes.

Test focus

This paper tests the ability of candidates to apply their knowledge of the language system. Parts 1 and 4 focus on both grammar and vocabulary; Parts 2 and 3 focus primarily on vocabulary and Part 5 focuses on an awareness of the use of language and summary writing skills.

Paper 3 outline

Part	Task type and focus	Number of questions	Task format
1	Open cloze Grammatical/lexico-grammatical	15	A text containing fifteen gaps. Each gap corresponds to a word. Candidates must write the missing word.
2	Word formation Lexical	10	A text containing ten gaps. Each gap corresponds to a word. The stems of the missing words are given beside the text and must be transformed to provide the missing word.

3	Gapped sentences Lexical (e.g. collocation, phrasal verbs, idioms, patterns in which lexical items occur)	6	Questions are made up of three discrete sentences. Each sentence contains one gap. The gapped word is common to the three sentences. Candidates must write one word which is appropriate in all three sentences.
4	Key word transformations Lexical/lexico-grammatical	8	Discrete items with a lead-in sentence and a gapped response to complete using a given word.
5	Comprehension questions and summary writing task Question focus: awareness of use of language (recognising and understanding the force of lexical items, rhetorical and stylistic devices and referencing) Summary tests information selection, linking, sentence construction	4 questions on the texts and 1 summary writing task	Two texts with two questions on each text. The summary task requires selection of relevant information from both texts.

Marks

One mark is given for each correct answer in questions 1–25.
Two marks are given for each correct answer in questions 26–31.
Up to two marks may be awarded for questions 32–39.
Two marks are given for each correct answer in questions 40–43.
Fourteen marks are available for question 44. Up to four marks may be awarded for content and ten for summary writing skills. The ten marks for summary writing skills are divided into five bands using the summary mark scheme.

Summary assessment

An impression mark for summary skills is awarded using a mark scheme with criteria describing performance in terms of the relevance, coherence, organisation, rewording and linguistic accuracy of the answer. Each piece of writing is assigned to a band between 0 and 5, where 5 represents an outstanding realisation of the task and 0 a negligible attempt or no attempt at the task set.

Marking

Candidates record their answers on separate answer sheets which are processed by trained markers. The mark scheme is adjusted at the beginning of the marking procedure to take account of actual candidate performance and then finalised. Part 5 is marked by a panel of trained examiners monitored by Team Leaders and a Principal Examiner.

Paper 4   Listening

The CPE Listening paper contains four parts with 28 questions and is approximately 40 minutes in length. The instructions which begin each section of the Listening paper are written and spoken. They give the general context for the text and explain the task. Candidates write their answers on the question paper while listening. Five minutes are allowed at the end of the test for them to transfer their answers to an answer sheet.

Texts

Different text types appropriate to the particular test focus are used in each part of the paper. They may be any of the following types:

Monologues:
- documentaries/features
- instructions
- commentaries
- lectures
- news broadcasts
- public announcements
- publicity/advertisements
- reports
- speeches
- stories/anecdotes
- talks

Interacting speakers:
- chat
- conversation
- discussion
- interview
- scripted drama
- transaction

Each text is heard twice. Recordings contain a variety of accents corresponding to standard variants of English native speaker accent. Background sounds may be included before speaking begins, to provide contextual information.

Test focus

The tasks in the Listening paper test candidates' ability to:
- select the relevant information from the text required to perform a task
- understand the gist of a text and its overall function and message
- identify and distinguish fact and opinion
- infer underlying meaning
- identify participation and role of different speakers in the discourse
- recognise attitude

Paper 4 outline

Part	Task type and focus	Number of questions	Task format
1	Three-option multiple choice Gist, detail, main idea, function, purpose, topic, speaker, addressee, feeling, attitude, opinion	8	Four short extracts from monologues or texts involving interacting speakers with two questions per extract.
2	Sentence completion Specific information, stated opinion	9	Candidates complete gaps in sentences with information from a monologue or prompted monologue.
3	Four-option multiple choice Opinion, gist, detail, inference	5	A text involving interacting speakers (e.g. interview) with multiple-choice questions.
4	Three-way matching Stated and non-stated opinion, agreement and disagreement	6	Candidates match statements on a text to either of two speakers or to both when they express agreement.

Marks

One mark is given for each correct answer.

For security reasons, several versions of the Listening paper are used at each administration of the examination. All tests are constructed to equal levels of difficulty using statistical information obtained by pre-testing the tasks on students before the live examination. After tests have been taken, the performance of the candidates in each of the versions is compared and marks adjusted to compensate for any slight imbalance in levels of difficulty.

Marking

Candidates record their answers on separate answer sheets which are processed by trained markers. The mark scheme for each version of the Listening paper is adjusted at the beginning of the marking procedure to take account of actual candidate performance.

Paper 5 Speaking

The CPE Speaking Test is conducted by two Oral Examiners (an Interlocutor and an Assessor) with pairs of candidates. The Interlocutor is responsible for conducting the Speaking Test and is also required to give a mark for each candidate's performance during the whole test. The Assessor is responsible for providing an analytical assessment of each candidate's performance and, after being introduced by the Interlocutor, takes no further part in the interaction. The Speaking Test takes 19 minutes for each pair of candidates and is divided into three parts.

NB The CPE Speaking Test is designed for pairs of candidates. However, where a centre has an uneven number of candidates, the last three candidates will be examined together. Oral Examiner packs contain shared tasks which are particularly appropriate for these groups of three. This test takes 28 minutes. Part 1 takes 4 minutes, Part 2 focus question – 2 minutes, decision-making task – 4 minutes, Part 3 – 18 minutes.

Test focus

The tasks in the Speaking Test require candidates to interact in conversational English in a range of contexts. Candidates demonstrate their ability to do this through appropriate control of grammar and vocabulary, discourse management, pronunciation and interactive communication.

Tasks

The paired format gives the opportunity for a range of interaction types – candidates speak to the Interlocutor in Part 1, to each other in Part 2, and to each other and the Interlocutor in Part 3. The three parts of the test are designed so that candidates deal with progressively more complex ideas and tasks, moving from personal topics to decision-making and discursive activities.

The focus of Part 1 is general interactional and social language. The Interlocutor asks each candidate three different questions, which require candidates to give information about themselves and to express personal opinions.

In Part 2 both candidates are involved in the same decision-making activity based on visual prompts. The candidates are first asked a question relating to one or more of the pictures. This introductory question gives candidates the chance to familiarise themselves with the topic and visuals before going on to the decision-making task. Candidates should be able to express their own opinions, invite the opinions and ideas of their partner and negotiate a decision.

In Part 3, the candidates speak on their own for two minutes, answering a question presented on a card. This gives them the opportunity to develop a topic individually, and to show their ability to sustain and organise a more extended contribution. The follow-up discussion allows candidates to explore the topics of the long turns in greater depth.

At the end of the Speaking Test, candidates are thanked for attending, but are given no indication of their level of achievement.

Paper 5 outline

Part	Task type and focus	Length of parts	Task format
1	Conversation between the Interlocutor and each candidate General interactional and social language	3 minutes	The Interlocutor encourages the candidates to give information about themselves and to express personal opinions.
2	Two-way conversation between the candidates Speculating, evaluating, comparing, giving opinions, decision making, etc.	4 minutes	The candidates are given visual and spoken prompts, which generate a discussion.
3	Long turn from each candidate followed by a discussion on topics related to the long turns	2 minute long turn for each candidate	Each candidate in turn is given a written question to respond to.
	Organising a larger unit of discourse, expressing and justifying opinions, developing topics	8 minutes following the long turns	Candidates engage in a discussion to explore further the topics of the long turns.

Assessment

Candidates are assessed on their own individual performance and not in relation to each other, according to the following analytical criteria: Grammatical Resource, Lexical Resource, Discourse Management, Pronunciation and Interactive Communication. These criteria are interpreted at CPE level. Assessment is based on performance in the whole test and is not related to particular parts of the test.

Both examiners assess the candidates. The Assessor applies detailed, analytical scales, and the Interlocutor applies the Global Achievement Scale, which is based on the analytical scales.

Grammatical Resource

This refers to the accurate application of grammar rules and the effective arrangement of words in utterances. At CPE level a wide range of structures should be used appropriately and competently.

Lexical Resource

This refers to the candidate's ability to use a wide and appropriate range of vocabulary to meet task requirements. At CPE level the tasks require candidates to express precise meanings, attitudes and opinions and to be able to convey abstract ideas. Although candidates may lack specialised vocabulary when dealing with unfamiliar topics, it should not in general terms be necessary to resort to simplification.

Discourse Management

This refers to the ability to link utterances together to form coherent monologue and contributions to dialogue. The utterances should be relevant to the tasks and to preceding utterances in the discourse. The discourse produced should be at a level of complexity appropriate to CPE level and the utterances should be arranged logically to develop the themes or arguments required by the tasks. The extent of contributions should be appropriate, i.e. long or short as required at a particular point in the dynamic development of the discourse in order to achieve the task.

Pronunciation

This refers to the ability to produce easily comprehensible utterances. Articulation of individual sounds is not required to be native speaker-like but should be sufficiently clear for all words to be easily understood. An acceptable rhythm of connected speech should be achieved by the appropriate use of strong and weak syllables, the smooth linking of words and the effective highlighting of information-bearing words. Intonation, which includes the use of a sufficiently wide pitch range and the appropriate use of contours, should be used effectively to convey meaning.

Interactive Communication

This refers to the ability to take an active part in the development of the discourse, showing sensitivity to turn taking and without undue hesitation. It requires the ability to participate competently in the range of interactive situations in the test and to develop discussions on a range of topics by initiating and responding appropriately. It also refers to the deployment of strategies to maintain and repair interaction at an appropriate level throughout the test so that the tasks can be fulfilled.

Global Achievement Scale

This refers to the candidate's overall performance throughout the test.

Throughout the Speaking Test candidates are assessed on their language skills and in order to be able to make a fair and accurate assessment of each candidate's performance, the examiners must be given an adequate sample of language to assess. Candidates must, therefore, be prepared to provide full answers to the questions asked by either the Interlocutor or the other candidate, and to speak clearly and audibly. While it is the responsibility of the Interlocutor, where necessary, to manage or direct the interaction, thus ensuring that both candidates are given an equal opportunity to speak, it is the responsibility of the candidates to maintain the interaction as much as possible. Candidates who take equal turns in the interchange will utilise to best effect the amount of time available.

Marking

After initial training, Oral Examiners are required to attend co-ordination sessions to maintain standardisation of marking. These sessions involve watching and discussing sample Speaking Tests recorded on video, and then conducting mock tests with volunteer candidates. The sample tests on video are selected to demonstrate a range of task types and different levels of competence, and are pre-marked by a team of experienced Oral Examiners.

In many countries, Oral Examiners are assigned to teams, each of which is led by a Team Leader who may be responsible for approximately fifteen Oral Examiners. Team Leaders give advice and support and also monitor Oral Examiners on a regular basis during live tests. The Team Leaders are responsible to a Senior Team Leader within their country, who is the professional representative of UCLES for the oral examinations. Senior Team Leaders are appointed by UCLES and attend annual co-ordination and development sessions in the UK. Team Leaders are appointed by the Senior Team Leader in consultation with the local administration.

Grading and results

Grading takes place once all scripts have been returned to UCLES and marking is complete. This is approximately six weeks after the examination. There are two main stages: grading and awards.

Grading

The five CPE papers total 200 marks, after weighting. Each paper represents 20% of the total marks available.

The overall grade boundaries (A, B, C, D and E) are set using the following information:

- statistics on the candidature
- statistics on the overall candidate performance
- statistics on individual items, for those parts of the examination for which this is appropriate (Papers 1, 3 and 4)
- the advice of the Chief Examiners, based on the performance of candidates, and on the recommendation of examiners where this is relevant (Paper 2 and Paper 3 Part 5)
- comparison with statistics from previous years' examination performance and candidature

A candidate's overall CPE grade is based on the total score gained by the candidate in all five papers. It is not necessary to achieve a satisfactory level in all five papers in order to pass the examination.

Awards

The Awarding Committee deals with all cases presented for special consideration, e.g. temporary disability, unsatisfactory examination conditions, suspected collusion, etc. The committee can decide to ask for scripts to be remarked, to check results, to change grades, to withhold results, etc. Results may be withheld because of infringement of regulations or because further investigation is needed. Centres are notified if a candidate's results have been scrutinised by the Awarding Committee.

Results

Results are reported as three passing grades (A, B and C) and two failing grades (D and E). The minimum successful performance which a candidate typically requires in order to achieve a grade C corresponds to about 60% of the total marks. Candidates are given statements of results which, in addition to their grades, show a graphical profile of their performance on each paper. These are shown against the scale Exceptional — Good — Borderline — Weak and indicate the candidate's relative performance in each paper. Certificates are issued to passing candidates after the issue of statements of results and there is no limit on the validity of the certificate.

Paper 2 sample answers and examiner's comments

Sample A (Test 1 Question 1)

> Nowadays were everything depends on technology many people work day and night to make a living and have no time for their family and that often causes many problems. Whoever lives in big cities breaths the polluted air from the factories. All these things harms their health and that is one of the reasons that city dwellers are facinated by the idea of the country.
>
> Everybody thinks that life is rosy in the country.
>
> The cleaner air, the big open places and the time they can spend with their family just exites them. But once they get there they're ready to leave again. What's the cause of that?
>
> Well the countryside like everything else in this world has its good and its bad points. The good point have been refered to above. The bad points are not many but they still exist.
>
> Everything is away from the great outdoors and if someone gets sick they can't get to the hospital emediately. It's not easy to go to the supermarket and go shopping and sometimes in winter when the weather is bad the road are often closed and you can't travell. The people who are used to fancy houses and easy lives if they decide to move to the country have to forget that and start living simpler and hubler.
>
> In conclusion do you realy think that moving to the countryside is such a good idea after all?

Comments

Content
The candidate has referred to the points raised in the question, often by merely repeating the wording, and there is little attempt to add any personal opinion.

Range
The range of expression and vocabulary is very limited.

Accuracy
There are errors of many kinds – in the use of structures, in agreement and in spelling. In some places the inaccuracies impede communication.

Appropriacy of register and format
The register is somewhat inconsistent and slips from formal to chatty. The rhetorical questions are inappropriately used.

Organisation and cohesion
The article is poorly organised, and the paragraphs are short and undeveloped.

Target reader
This is a poor attempt at the task and has a very negative effect on the reader.

Band 1

Sample B (Test 1 Question 3)

Last August the theatre group of the high school of Eginis took part in the International Festival of Drama which took place in Nicosia, Cyprus. The play we performed was called 'The life of Socrates' and was based on the life of the great philosophist.

Our team was composed of twenty student-actors, the school's two philologists and of course the headmaster. We were hosted at the four-star hotel during the festival which lasted three weeks. The guide agency which took over our entertainment had programmed some tours at museums and archeological places. Fifty schools from twenty six countries took place. We were the only school from Greece and that's why we chose to perform a play which was relevant to our country's history. The play talks about Socrate's life and teaching. It included many of his most important speeches. It came to a summit when Socrates drunk the poison the guardians gave him while he was in prison despite his students attempts to talk him into escaping and leaving Athens. I played the part of John. One of Socrates best student and friend who had planned how his teacher was going to escape if he wanted to.

Surpassing my expectations it was a great success as we finally took the first place. The audience was amazed. It stopped applauding only when we left the theatre. But the most moving moment was when a Turkish group, which took the nineteenth place came to our hotel and congratulated us. They stayed there for about three hours joining our party. When they finally left they invited us to visit their school and we told that we would be glad to.

During our flight back to Greece we were very happy for our success. We were glaring our gold medals and couldn't wait to show them to our parents and schoolmates. But we couldn't forget the organizers' hospitality. We all learnt that we can achieve a goal, however difficult it may seem, by hard work. And that even if you don't achieve it you shouldn't be worried. On the contrary you should be happy only because you did your best.

Comments

Content
All the points referred to in the question have been well covered.

Range
There is an adequate range of structure and vocabulary.

Accuracy
There are some errors and there is some awkward expression (*we were very happy for our success*), but the meaning is always clear.

Appropriacy of register and format
The answer is in appropriate format for a review, and the register is consistent.

Organisation and cohesion
The review is well organised. The subject is clearly introduced in the first paragraph, and there is an appropriate conclusion.

Target reader
This is a satisfactory realisation of the task. The reader would have a clear understanding of the festival, and what it meant to the students.

Band 3

Sample C (Test 1 Question 4)

Dear new students

    We would like to welcome you all, to our college. We are going to try to make you feel as well as possible without treating you like strangers. Also, we're going to inform you about the college facilities and guide you on the clubs, the societies and the student services, that exist.

    Firstly, the canteen provides cheap snacks and drinks and we'd suggest to use it as much as possible. Furthermore, we believe that it is essential for you to be aware of the size of our library. It can be incredibly useful during your studies, so that's why you should try to make the best use of it. Moreover, the IT suite is always open to the students who would like to use the computers for researches or projects. You should also know about the college's big sports hall, which could help you to keep yourselves fit. Finally, another useful facility is the cinema where you can entertain yourselves for free every Friday and Saturday only.

    It is also very important for you to know about the clubs, the societies and the student services that exist in our college. Firstly there is an excellent soccer club for the ones that like to play soccer and there is a computer club for the persons who like and know how to use computers. Moreover, the literature society is very popular to the students who love the work of foreign poets and writers. We believe you should also be informed about the art society where students gather up and share their own work with each other. So if you think you are talented in painting or in any other kind of art, don't hesitate to join in. Finally, it is very important for you to know about a very useful student service, the laundry. But you're obliged to pay some money in order to have access to it.

    We hope that these informations will aid you, and we'd like to let you know that you should always feel welcome to ask any questions you may have.

Comments

Content
The content is relevant and the candidate has referred to the aspects of college life mentioned in the question.

Range
The range of vocabulary, structures and expression is limited.

Accuracy
There are few serious errors, but the language lacks fluency and there is some awkward and unnatural expression – *But you're obliged to pay some money in order to have access to it.*

Appropriacy of register and format
The answer is in appropriate letter format, and the register is consistent.

Organisation and cohesion
The letter is well organised and paragraphed.

Target reader
Despite the stilted expression, the candidate has managed to write a welcoming and helpful letter, but this is an inadequate attempt at the task because of the inaccuracies in language.

Band 2

Sample D (Test 1 Question 5c)

Dear Sir or Madam

English literature of the 20th century dealt with many different topics and revealed a variety of characters but did it not provide us with any heroes? I would like to respond to this statement, based on your article about English literature of the twentieth century, by referring to G.Greene's main character named Wormold in "Our Man in Havana".

Why do we call a person a hero? Because of being brave, helpful, reliable, or having done something extraordinary? Relating to these attributes, Wormold can easily be called a hero.

He shows bravery with his attempts to warn at least two of his so-called agents. Moreover, I am sure that he is helpful to his daughter Milly or Dr Hasselbacher and they can rely on him, as well. Spying or inventing reports and stories can also be described as something extraordinary. Therefore, Wormold achieves the status of a hero. But is he a hero throughout Greene's novel and are his heroic acts really helpful for anybody?

In this case, the answer has to be "no". Neither does Wormold act heroic in the whole novel nor does he really help anybody with his attempts. In fact, he even worsens most situations because of his behaviour.

In my opinion, Wormold wants to be a hero for his daughter and, therefore, he starts being brave and doing extraordinary things, but these heroic attributes are not really characteristics of Wormold himself. He rather has to develop them because of exterior circumstances, as well as his desire to make his daughter's wishes come true. According to this, he only acts heroic when his spy-career is in danger.

Moreover, I believe that Wormold never faced the consequences of being "an agent", nor did he show any real affection -at the beginning- when his whole invented story got out of control.

Therefore, based on Greene's novel, I would agree with your statement.

However, in my opinion, heroes are not made by outstanding circumstances, they rather act heroic because they think of others, first, instead of their own profit.

Yours sincerely

Comments

Content
The letter attempts to deal with the concept of heroism. There is just adequate reference to episodes and events in the novel.

Range
There is a reasonable range of vocabulary.

Accuracy
There are few errors in language, though there are instances of poor or awkward expression – *Greene's main character named* Wormold, *neither does Wormold act heroic.*

Appropriacy of register and format
The format is appropriate and the register consistent.

Organisation and cohesion
The letter lacks cohesion in places, but it is generally coherent.

Target reader
The target reader would have some idea of the writer's viewpoint.

Band 3

Sample E (Test 2 Question 3)

People from various backgrounds and with a different standard of education have been asked their opinion on what they would prefer the local money to be spent on. They had to choose among a new leisure centre, a new library or a new playground for children The result will be rather helpful for your decision.

A new leisure centre: The majority of the people argued that there is no real need for a new leisure centre. There are already enough of them and thus, increasing their number will only cause more noise. Moreover, since there is already limited space for parking around the vicinity, the new leisure centre will deteriorate the problem. There were also some parents who were afraid that their children will be carried away by the presence of another leisure centre.

A new library: Many people claimed that besides the existence of a few libraries in the town, none of them has enough space for the children to study there. The time which children spend at school is not enough for their enriching their knowledge. On the other hand, books have become too expensive. Consequently, only the minority of the parents has the ability to buy to their children all the books they need. A new library which will contain not only literary books, but also books about history, art or sciences seems ideal.

A new playground for children: Opinions on this suggeston were sharply divided. Everyone who was for the building of the new playground for children, would suggest that it should be built in their own vicinity. The rest of the people who had been asked, recommended that a new library would be preferable to the playground, since books are difficult to be obtained and knowledge needs much time to be gained.

Conclusion: It is obvious that the majority would be satisfied by a new library, even if they disagree at the time. Besides we are well aware of the fact that parents are more eager to spend time on studying rather than playing. Last but not least, we should take for granted that everybody will be benefited from the new library no matter what their age is.

Comments

Content
The candidate has included all the information specified in the question and drawn an appropriate conclusion.

Range
The candidate has used an adequate range of vocabulary, structures and expression.

Accuracy
There are a few non-impeding errors in expression – *to choose among, will deteriorate the problem.*

Appropriacy of register and format
The format is appropriate to a report with good use of headings. The register is consistent.

Organisation and cohesion
The answer is well organised with a clear introduction and conclusion.

Target reader
This is a satisfactory realisation of the task. The report is well organised and businesslike, and the reader would have a clear understanding of the views expressed.

Band 3

Sample F (Test 2 Question 4)

When I visited Italy during last summer, I realised that it is one of the most unexplored counties in Europe. This opinion of mine may seem strange since Italy attracts millions of tourists every year, but I am sure that most of them are not able to appreciate the true beauty of this country, which hides pleasant surprises and mysteries in every part.

Of course we are all familiar with places in Italy like Venice or Verona. The possibility of your having visited towns like Pisa or 'Firenze' is very high. Even if one hadn't had the chance to go to Italy and admire the beautiful architecture or the old buildings which can be seen in these cities, there are many programmes on every television channel that give one the opportunity to become familiar with the famous sights of this country. It is certain that we all agree that going to Venice, the sinking city, or to Verona, the city where Romeo and Julliette lived their love and died for it, is a very romantic experience. Let us not forget also that this is the place that gave birth to many scientists and artists, like Leonardo da Vinci, whose contribution to the progress of the human race is priceless.

But there is another part of Italy, equally magnificent, but not so well known. And that is the southern part of Italy, which until recently was thought of as 'the poor Italy'. In this area the visitor will not have the chance to admire beautiful Catholic churches or gigantic buildings as in the north. But this area is suited to tourists who prefer relaxing during their vacation and avoiding crowded places. There are many traditional villages which are usually built on the slopes of a hill, and as you can imagine the view of the Mediterranean sea is extraordinary. The beaches are covered with gold sand and the sea is crystal clear and a beautiful green colour. It is not easy to find a big luxurious hotel, but in every village there are small traditional hotels that will satisfy most of your needs. The people are very friendly and their simplicity may surprise you. And if you look hard enough, you may discover many ancient Greek temples, which are sometimes very well preserved, but unfortunately neglected.

So it is easy to realise that Italy can satisfy any desire a tourist may have. Do you want to visit a beautiful country and are not worried by crowded streets? Then visit northern Italy. But if you want to relax and enjoy calmness and serenity, I definitely suggest that you should vist the southern part of Italy, the unexplored Italy.

Comments

Content

As the question asks, the candidate describes two contrasting aspects of Italy, and encourages the reader to visit the country.

Range

The article uses a wide range of vocabulary and structures, and the language is fluent and natural.

Accuracy

There is minimal error – a couple of spelling mistakes, an incorrectly used preposition.

Appropriacy of register and format

The format is appropriate and the register is particularly suitable for a magazine article. The reader is addressed in a personal way.

Organisation and cohesion

The article is well organised and paragraphed.

Target reader

This is a very good realisation of the task. The reader would be interested, informed and encouraged to visit Italy, and the article would have a very positive effect.

Band 5

Sample G (Test 3 Question 1)

<u>Employment in the future</u>

Today's world of work is not easy at all. Some old work's methods have been replaced by innovations of the modern technology and global economy has created lots of job competition. So that the unemployment rate has increased and it doesn't seem that the situation will be better for the near future.

Things were different only 20 years ago, when jobs were more permanent and would accompany one's whole life.

Good education itself is not enough anymore because the competition of well-educated people is ruthless.

The challenge is big and so are also new opportunities.

The positive overcoming of the circumstances mostly depend on people's attitudes towards changes and progress.

New technologies bring new kind of employment. One good example would be internet, which has created new kind of jobs like for instance web designer.

New knowledge is required.

The more flexible people are, the more they can adapt themselves to the requirements of today's work. They must be able to transform changes into resources instead of considering them as threats.

People need to be more visionary and try to foresee in which direction new industries are developing and try keeping up with the times. There's a need of dynamic people, who can bring innovative ideas and creativity and who look at changes with a positive attitude. It is important to always be willing to learn something new, to gain new competence and improve it for the professional development. That attitude would not only bring a lot to one's personal growth, but would also help our society to keep its evolution.

Things won't change, there will always be unemployment in the future, but we won't have any reason to worry about it if we will be able to be contemporary of the future, to adapt ourselves to changes and to try to be continually enriched by them.

Comments

Content
The candidate has addressed the points raised in the question and developed these ideas.

Range
There is a good use of vocabulary and an adequate range of structure and expression.

Accuracy
There are some errors, but the meaning is clear, although expression is awkward and unnatural in some places – *the positive overcoming of the circumstances; for the near future.*

Appropriacy of register and format
The format is appropriate and the register consistent.

Organisation and cohesion
The essay is poorly paragraphed and, particularly in the first part, is merely a succession of unconnected though relevant points.

Target reader
This is a satisfactory realisation of the task. The reader would understand the writer's views, although these are not presented in a very well argued form.

Band 3

Sample H (Test 3 Question 4)

> ### GOOD NEIGHBOURS ARE WORTH
> ### THEIR WEIGHT IN GOLD
>
> *Do you believe that the word "neighbour" is a synonym to "nuisance"? Are you of the opinion that there is no such thing as "a good neighbour"? Do you think that a neighbour is someone who annoys you by listening to music at the highest pitch when you are taking a nap at noon? Or someone who watches your every move and spends his time gossiping with your other neighbours about you? Well, think again! There is such thing as good neighbours and if you are lucky enough to have them you ought to know that they are worth their weight in gold.*
>
> *I happen to be one of the lucky ones. My neighbours are very kind and warm people, always willing to help everyone in need. I have personal experience of their compassion and helpfulness. It was a year ago when my house flooded because of a sudden and very intense storm. The water kept coming in and my parents and I were unable to stop it. When the storm finally ended, we faced a total disaster. The water had covered all the rooms and it had reached the height of our knees. Our neighbour, who came to see if we needed any help, saw the situation and invited us to spend the night in her flat. That is what we did and the next morning our neighbour and her daughter helped us clean our house and put everything in order again. I will always remember that difficult situation, because despite our trouble, we realized the importance of good neighbours.*
>
> *Good neighbours are those who follow some simple rules of good manners and those who you trust and who are willing to watch over your house and take care of your plants when you are away on vacation. But most of all, good neighbours are those who are always ready to help you out whenever you need a hand and those who sympathize with you whenever you deal with a problem and rejoice at your happiness and success. Good neighbours are just as important as good friends and even more, because you can always count on them, since they live next to you.*
>
> *"A friend in need is a friend indeed", as the saying goes. Well, allow me to change it and say: "A neighbour in need is a neighbour indeed" and for that alone he is worth his weight in gold!*

Comments

Content
The candidate has done exactly what the question asked – related a personal experience and drawn some conclusions from it.

Range
The structures and vocabulary are suitable for the task.

Accuracy
There are few errors and these are minor instances of awkwardness in expression – *it had reached the height of our knees.*

Appropriacy of register and format
The register is particularly appropriate to the task. It is informal and speaks directly to the reader. The format is suited to a magazine article.

Organisation and cohesion
The article is well organised with a good introduction and conclusion.

Target reader
This is a good realisation of the task. It is an interesting article and would have a positive effect on the reader.

Band 4

Sample I (Test 4 Question 1)

Dear Sir or Madam

I am writing to make a proposal for the new fast food restaurant which may be build in the future in the historic centre of Baden.

I am the representative of the local student organisation SOB. The issue was hotly debated at the last meeting of the SOB. Finally, we came up with the following proposal in favour of the fast food restaurant. I would like to present you with the proposal.

The main advantage of a modern fast food restaurant is, that it will surely attract many young people. The young will then more often come to Baden. At the beginning, perhaps they are primarily interested in the restaurant, but certainly after a while they will show more interest in the local history due to the location of the restaurant. The culture of the city will be found just around the building, which helps the rather philistine people to get contact with the fascinating history of Baden.

From an architectural point of view it would be exciting place which would be worth seeing because of the strong contrast in style between the 15th century buildings and the modernism of the restaurant. Furthermore, it encourages also families to visit Baden. Nowadays we have only common restaurants where small children have not much fun and sometimes they are even not welcome. Whereas these fast food restaurants are always very child-friendly and they often have a playground area for children. Therefore it is no longer a problem for the parents to combine the satisfaction of their cultural desire with the one for their children. In addition, if the children then become familiar with their local history, their understanding and respect of the town will grow and develope and this can only have a positive effect when the children are grown-up.

In conclusion, the points mentioned before would all contribute to an increase of visitors and thus also the revenue of the town would raise. I believe Baden would benefit a lot from a new fast food restaurant in the historic centre.

I am looking forward to hear from you about your position to our proposal.

Yours faithfully,

Comments

Content

The candidate has covered the points raised in the question and presented a clear argument.

Range

The proposal shows a range of vocabulary and structures, and there is some good use of natural expression – *hotly debated; we came up with the following proposal; strong contrast.*

Accuracy

There are only minor errors in expression – *respect of the town; looking forward to hear from you* – and the meaning is always clear.

Appropriacy of register and format

The proposal has been suitably organised within the format of a letter. The register is consistent and appropriate.

Organisation and cohesion

The proposal is well organised and paragraphed.

Target reader

This is a good realisation of the task. The reader would have a clear idea of the writer's views.

Band 4

Sample J (Test 4 Question 2)

KUALA LUBUR THE IDEAL PLACE FOR YOUR HOLIDAY

Going on holidays does not always entail having fun and amusing yourself. It often depends on the place you visit, the people that accompany you, the duration of the holiday or even the money you are going to spend.

Kuala Lubur, in Asia, exemplifies the perfect place for an adventurous holiday. The climate is quite tropical. During the day the weather is hot, but during the night it is rainy. As far as the nature is concerned, there are endless landscapes of gorgeous valleys with lakes or rivers and vast green tropical forests which provide the chance of exploration or inner relaxation. The area is spotted with picteresque villages and small towns where people live blithely in unison. The Asian folk is exceptional. Its simplicity, its hospitality and its warmth allow everyone to acquaint with them despite the difference in language. People are trully friendly and kind. In terms of civilisation, they have various traditions and customs, which are worth knowing. They often do rituals in their temples for their gods and godeses, for whom they are always ready to sacrifice even themselves.

A group of thirty students from our school – including me, the writer – had the opportunity to visit Kuala Lubur; and we would now like to inform you about this trip, which lasted ten days.. Exploring all the area, visiting different places, meeting other – different – people, we found ourselves amazed by their culture, their mentality, their hospitality and their lifestyle. Everything, even the nature itself, enchanted, captivated us, while it "subconsciously" invited us to the adventure of its exploration.

Indisputably Kuala Lubur constitutes the ideal place for your holidays, combining a low cost with endless adventure and amusement. We recommend it to all of you, as it is worth visiting more than once.

Comments

Content
The candidate has described an unusual holiday destination, but has not really dealt adequately with the idea of an 'adventure' holiday.

Range
The range of structure and expression is limited.

Accuracy
There are few serious errors, but the expression is often awkward and inappropriate – *where people live blithely in unison; the Asian folk*.

Appropriacy of register and format
The register is consistent, but this is a poor attempt at a review format.

Organisation and cohesion
The answer is poorly organised. The candidate begins with a general description of the place visited, and does not explain what exactly is being reviewed until more than half way through the piece of writing. Cohesion is poor, and there is considerable repetition.

Target reader
This is an inadequate attempt at the task and would have a negative effect on the reader.

Band 2

Paper 3 summary answers and examiner's comments

Sample A (Test 1)

> Business success nowdays is put down to people who can couple intelligence with a strong character decided to stay ahead in the race and not just follow the changes and needs of today. In the same way athletics is important to an athlete as well as his physical strength. But those intellegent, ambitious people work even efficiently while joining their efforts in a work team just like happening in a sport team where individuals can correct, support, others and provide solutions and improvements.

Comments

Content points: (i), (ii), (iii)

The reader is adequately informed by this paragraph which, although somewhat overlength (83 words), is generally relevant, reasonably coherent, adequately organised and makes some use of linking devices. Its weaknesses are a number of errors in grammar, spelling and expression, as well as inaccurate punctuation, which to some extent impede communication.

Content: 3 marks

Summary skills: Band 3

Sample B (Test 1)

> The difference between success in business and in sport is that in a business you have to work as team in order to become "a big name" in your subject. On the other hand, in sport you, also, have to work as a whole, but you can become a superstar by your own talent in football, for example.

Comments

Content points: (iii)

This attempt shows little evidence of summary skills as it fails to inform the reader of the subject matter of the two texts. Although quite short, it is mostly irrelevant, poorly expressed and contains grammatical inaccuracies, e.g. in the misuse of the indefinite article.

Content: 1 mark

Summary skills: Band 1

Sample C (Test 2)

> *There are many factors that can lead people to explore the countryside. First of all a wild place is by itself a great challenge to them like the extreme sports which raise their adrenaline. They are usually lonely and ramble as they don't want to be with others. Rambling in the countryside provides them fresh air and also makes them more self-confident which results in their independance. Finally they have new experiences which means more skills and more self-esteem.*

Comments

Content points: (i), (ii), (iii), (iv)

The summary is relevant, well organised, uses appropriate linking devices and requires minimal effort on the part of the reader. It is marred somewhat by a slight awkwardness of expression and by non-impeding errors in spelling and punctuation.

Content: 4 marks

Summary skills: Band 4

Sample D (Test 2)

> *People want to explore the countryside so as to avoid smoking or being phanatic about teams. Another reason is because they become depressed of the so many buildings around them and the lack of fresh air. According to recent research hikers go to the countryside because there they can be alone as they want. Except from hikers, people who want to find peace and relief of tention from the city go for walks to nature because it is believed that their self-esteem would be improved. Also people find spiritual uplift there. Finally people explore the countryside because they don't get satisfaction from city's facilities because of the pollution.*

Comments

Content points: (i), (iii), (iv)

This summary requires considerable effort on the part of the reader due to irrelevance, poor expression and excessive length (108 words). It shows some attempt at organisation, but suffers seriously from linguistic errors such as repeated misuse of prepositions, wrong tenses and spelling mistakes, all of which impede communication.

Content: 3 marks

Summary skills: Band 2

Sample E (Test 3)

> *People are able to perceive the world through the five senses, however, not all stimuli are allowed to be received. If every signal was to be let in this would lead to people's unability to make out object affecting their survival – owing to the wide range of light waves – or to their confusion because of the variety of sounds that are ugly if one could listen to so as to be unable to react to sounds he is in need of.*

Comments

Content points: (ii), (iii)

The summary informs adequately, but requires some effort on the part of the reader. Though adequately organised, it makes little use of linking devices. It contains several linguistic errors, some of which impede communication, and the second sentence is too long and badly constructed. Overall it just fulfils the criteria for Band 3.

Content: 2 marks

Summary skills: Band 3

Sample F (Test 3)

> *If our senses enabled us to perceive everything we wouldn't be able to tell the difference between objects, even those that are essential to our survival. In addition we would be forced to hear all sounds, both the melodic and the defeaning ones, and therefore prevented from hearing the most important sounds. To make a long story short, our lives would be a mess and our species at risk.*

Comments

Content points: (ii), (iii), (iv)

The paragraph supplies most of the relevant information with minimal effort required from the reader. It is concise, coherent, well organised and attempts to use linking devices. It is linguistically fluent and accurate, except for inappropriately used vocabulary in the final sentence.

Content: 3 marks

Summary skills: Band 4

Sample G (Test 4)

> *Relying on technology sustains our life much convinient and business-like. However it depends on the situations. We still love, and feel confortable using basic civilizations such as pencils and so on. Technology might cause a social problem like job-shortage, it could be continuing. But, as far as the invention is made by human, we can think about the situations. Those problem will not be worse.*

Comments

Content points: (iv)

This answer partially informs but requires considerable effort on the part of the reader. Although concise, it shows some irrelevance and only limited use of linking devices. The quality of the language is inadequate due to incorrect vocabulary and a number of errors in grammar and spelling which sometimes impede communication.

Content: 1 mark

Summary skills: Band 2

Sample H (Test 4)

> *Some people predict that new technologies will change the way of living, for instance unemployment will be increased, which was occured in early 19th century. However, this prediction can be wrong. The jobs, which were extinguished by technology, have been replaced by another jobs and in higher volume. Besides, some certain things can not be changed by new technology because they perfectly suit for their function.*

Comments

Content points: (i), (ii), (iii), (iv)

The reader is clearly informed by this summary which is totally relevant, concise, coherent, skilfully organised and uses appropriate connectors. Although fluently written and correctly punctuated, it contains various non-impeding errors in grammar and vocabulary which place it in Band 4.

Content: 4 marks

Summary skills: Band 4

Paper 5 frameworks

Test 1

Note: In the examination, there will be both an Assessor and an Interlocutor in the room.

The visual material for Part 2 is on pages C2 and C3 in the colour section of the Student's Book. The prompt cards for Part 3 are on pages C10 and C11 in the colour section of the Student's Book.

Part 1 (3 minutes)

Interlocutor:	Good morning/afternoon. My name is .... and this is my colleague .... And your names are .... ?
Candidates:	....
Interlocutor:	Thank you. Could I have your mark sheets, please?
	Now, first of all, it would be nice to find out something about each of you.
	Where are you from, (*Candidate A*)? And you, (*Candidate B*)?
	Select a further question for each candidate.

- What are you doing at the moment?
- Do you enjoy your work / your studies?
- What's the best thing about the area that you come from?
- Why did you decide to learn English?
- What other languages do you think would be useful for you?

Candidates A & B:	....
Interlocutor:	*Select a further question for each candidate.*

- Can you tell us something about what your work or studies involve?
- Can you tell us something about the neighbourhood you live in?
- What could you recommend to do in the evenings where you live?
- What holiday destinations would you recommend in your country?
- Could you tell us where you like to go when you need to relax?
- And what about your interests? How important is music to you?

Candidates A & B:	....

Interlocutor:	Thank you. Now, we'd like to ask you what you think about one or two things.

Select one more question for each candidate.

- On the subject of leisure, how important is TV in your culture?
- If you could choose to have a talent for something, what would it be?
- On the subject of studying, how have you used technology in your education?
- Thinking about education, do you think university students should have to earn money while studying?
- Where would you most like to go if you were offered a dream holiday?
- Moving on to the future, what aspect excites you most?

Candidates A & B:	....
Interlocutor:	Thank you.

Part 2 (4 minutes)   *Conference programme – Pressures at work*

Interlocutor:	Now, in this part of the test you're going to do something together. Here are some pictures of people at work.

Place the picture sheet for Test 1 in front of the candidates.

First, I'd like you to look at pictures *and* (*Select from pictures A–G*) and talk together about how the people in the pictures might be feeling about their work.

You have about a minute for this, so don't worry if I interrupt you.

Candidates A & B:	[*One minute.*]
Interlocutor:	Thank you. Now, look at all the pictures. I'd like you to imagine that a health organisation is planning a conference programme on pressures at work.

Talk together about what aspects of pressure at work are represented in the pictures. Two of these issues will have to be excluded from the conference programme because of lack of time. Decide which two to exclude.

You have about three minutes to talk about this.

Candidates A & B:	[*Three minutes.*]
Interlocutor:	Thank you. *Retrieve picture sheet.*

Part 3   (12 minutes)   *The past*

Interlocutor:	Now, in this part of the test you're each going to talk on your own for about two minutes. You need to listen while your partner is speaking because you'll be asked to comment afterwards.

So, (*Candidate A*), I'm going to give you a card with a question written on it and I'd like you to tell us what you think. There are also some ideas on the card for you to use if you like.

All right? Here is your card, and a copy for you, (*Candidate B*).

Hand over a copy of prompt card 1a to each candidate.

Remember, (*Candidate A*), you have about two minutes to talk before we join in.

[*Allow up to 10 seconds before saying, if necessary:* Would you like to begin now?]

Candidate A: [*Two minutes.*]

Interlocutor: Thank you.

*Select **one** appropriate follow-up question for Candidate B.*

- What do you think?
- Is there anything you would like to add?
- Is there anything you don't agree with?
- How does this differ from your experience?

Candidate B: [*One minute.*]

Interlocutor: *Address **one** of the following questions to both candidates.*

- Should it be compulsory to study history at school?
- How could learning about history be made more appealing to young people?
- Why is it important to study the history of other countries?

Candidates
A & B: [*One minute.*]

Interlocutor: Thank you. *Retrieve cards.*

Now (*Candidate B*), it's your turn to be given a question.

Hand over a copy of prompt card 1b to both candidates.

Here is your card, and a copy for you, (*Candidate A*). Remember, (*Candidate B*), you have about two minutes to tell us what you think, and there are some ideas on the card for you to use if you like. All right?

[*Allow up to 10 seconds before saying, if necessary:* Would you like to begin now?]

Candidate B: [*Two minutes.*]

Interlocutor: Thank you.

*Select **one** appropriate follow-up question for Candidate A.*

- What do you think?
- Is there anything you would like to add?
- Is there anything you don't agree with?
- How does this differ from your experience?

Candidate A:	[*One minute.*]
Interlocutor:	*Address **one** of the following questions to both candidates.*

- Do you think daily life was easier or more difficult in past times?
- Would you like to have lived in an earlier time?
- Why do people collect things from the past?

Candidates A & B:	[*One minute.*]
Interlocutor:	Thank you. *Retrieve cards.*

Interlocutor:	Now, to finish the test, we're going to talk about the past in general.

Address a selection of the following questions to both candidates.

- Does history focus too much on the lives of the famous?
- Do you think we learn more from achievements or mistakes of the past?
- Which has changed the world more – science or politics?
- How easy is it to keep traditions alive? Does it matter if they die?
- Which figure from history would you most like to have met?
- How do you think this period of time will be remembered in the future?

Candidates A & B:	[*Four minutes.*]
Interlocutor:	Thank you. That is the end of the test.

Test 2

Note: In the examination, there will be both an Assessor and an Interlocutor in the room.

The visual material for Part 2 is on pages C4 and C5 in the colour section of the Student's Book. The prompt cards for Part 3 are on pages C10 and C11 in the colour section of the Student's Book.

Part 1   (3 minutes)

Interlocutor: Good morning/afternoon. My name is .... and this is my colleague .... And your names are .... ?

Candidates: ....

Interlocutor: Thank you. Could I have your mark sheets, please?

Now, first of all, it would be nice to find out something about each of you.

Where are you from, (*Candidate A*)? And you, (*Candidate B*)?

Select a further question for each candidate.

- What are you doing at the moment?
- Do you enjoy your work / your studies?
- What's the best thing about the area that you come from?
- What do you like about learning English?
- Is there anything you don't like about your work or your studies?

Candidates A & B: ....

Interlocutor: *Select a further question for each candidate.*

- Given a choice, would you rather learn another language or a different skill?
- When you have free time, what do you most enjoy doing?
- What's your opinion of the leisure facilities in the area where you live?
- Let's move on to holidays. What makes a holiday a success for you?
- What about food? Are you a good cook?
- What do you think you'll be doing in say 10 years' time?

Candidates A & B: ....

Interlocutor: Thank you. Now, we'd like to ask you what you think about one or two things.

*Select **one** more question for each candidate.*

- How important is it, do you think, to have a hobby?
- What do you most hope to achieve using your language skills?
- Thinking about your education, which teacher (has) made the biggest impression on you?
- Thinking about where you live, how important are your surroundings to you?
- What advice would you give to someone who is thinking of moving to your area?
- Moving on to current affairs, do you keep up with the news? How?

Candidates A & B:	....
Interlocutor:	Thank you.

Part 2 (4 minutes)   *Environmental campaign – Local transport*

Interlocutor: Now, in this part of the test you're going to do something together. Here are some pictures connected with transport.

Place the picture sheet for Test 2 in front of the candidates.

First, I'd like you to look at pictures *and* (*Select from pictures A–G*) and talk together about how traffic affects our lives.

You have about a minute for this, so don't worry if I interrupt you.

Candidates A & B: [*One minute.*]

Interlocutor: Thank you. Now, look at all the pictures. I'd like you to imagine that an environmental pressure group is planning a campaign to focus attention on making local transport systems more environmentally friendly.

Talk together about the issues suggested in these pictures and then decide which two issues the campaign should focus on.

You have about three minutes to talk about this.

Candidates A & B: [*Three minutes.*]

Interlocutor: Thank you. *Retrieve picture sheet.*

Part 3 (12 minutes)   *Change and development*

Interlocutor: Now, in this part of the test you're going to talk on your own for about two minutes. You need to listen while your partner is speaking because you'll be asked to comment afterwards.

So, (*Candidate A*), I'm going to give you a card with a question written on it and I'd like you to tell us what you think. There are also some ideas on the card for you to use if you like.

All right? Here is your card, and a copy for you, (*Candidate B*).

Hand over a copy of prompt card 2a to each candidate.

Remember, (*Candidate A*), you have about two minutes to talk before we join in.

[*Allow up to 10 seconds before saying, if necessary:* Would you like to begin now?]

Candidate A: [*Two minutes.*]

Interlocutor: Thank you.

*Select **one** appropriate follow-up question for Candidate B.*

- What do you think?
- Is there anything you would like to add?
- Is there anything you don't agree with?
- How does this differ from your experience?

Candidate B: [*One minute.*]

Interlocutor: *Address **one** of the following questions to both candidates.*

- Why do you think some people find change difficult?
- What technological development would you like to see in the next 30 years?
- How can busy working people keep up with changes in technology?

Candidates
A & B: [*One minute.*]

Interlocutor: Thank you. *Retrieve cards.*

Now, (*Candidate B*), it's your turn to be given a question.

Hand over a copy of prompt card 2b to both candidates.

Here is your card, and a copy for you, (*Candidate A*). Remember, (*Candidate B*), you have about two minutes to tell us what you think, and there are some ideas on the card for you to use if you like. All right?

[*Allow up to 10 seconds before saying, if necessary:* Would you like to begin now?]

Candidate B: [*Two minutes.*]

Interlocutor: Thank you.

*Select **one** appropriate follow-up question for Candidate A.*

- What do you think?
- Is there anything you would like to add?
- Is there anything you don't agree with?
- How does this differ from your experience?

Candidate A: [*One minute.*]

Interlocutor: *Address **one** of the following questions to both candidates.*

- How do you think the world's languages will change in the future?
- Do you welcome changes in your language?
- How can we prevent languages dying out?

Candidates
A & B: [*One minute.*]

Interlocutor: Thank you. *Retrieve cards.*

Interlocutor: Now, to finish the test, we're going to talk about change and development in general.

                Address a selection of the following questions to both candidates.

- Why do you think each generation wants to be different?
- What do you feel has been the most positive development in your lifetime?
- What impact has mass air travel had on the way we view the world?
- Are there some things about life or people that don't change? Do you think this will continue?
- When do you think a child changes to being an adult?
- When is change necessary? And when is it a luxury?

Candidates
A & B: [*Four minutes.*]

Interlocutor: Thank you. That is the end of the test.

Test 3

Note: In the examination, there will be both an Assessor and an Interlocutor in the room.

The visual material for Part 2 is on pages C6 and C7 in the colour section of the Student's Book. The prompt cards for Part 3 are on pages C10 and C11 in the colour section of the Student's Book.

Part 1   (3 minutes)

Interlocutor:	Good morning/afternoon. My name is .... and this is my colleague .... And your names are .... ?
Candidates:	....
Interlocutor:	Thank you. Could I have your mark sheets, please?
	Now, first of all, it would be nice to find out something about each of you.
	Where are you from, (*Candidate A*)? And you, (*Candidate B*)?
	Select a further question for each candidate.

- What are you doing at the moment?
- Do you enjoy your work / your studies?
- What's the best thing about the area that you come from?
- Has the area where you live changed much in your lifetime?
- Would you be happy to live in the same place all your life?

Candidates A & B:	....
Interlocutor:	*Select a further question for each candidate.*

- What is there to do in your free time where you live?
- How easy is it to get to interesting places from where you live?
- Could you tell us something about the things you enjoy reading?
- What about music? Do you prefer live concerts or recorded music?
- What would you say has been your best experience this year?
- What are your plans for the next 2 or 3 years?

Candidates A & B:	....
Interlocutor:	Thank you. Now, we'd like to ask you what you think about one or two things.
	*Select **one** more question for each candidate.*

- Which language do you think a foreigner would find more difficult to learn – yours or English?
- In your opinion, what's the best way to use your free time?

- Do you think you'll still be doing the same things in your free time in 10 or 20 years' time?
- If you could live anywhere in the world, where would it be?
- Thinking about friends, what do you think makes a good friend?
- How do you think our working lives will change in your lifetime?

Candidates A & B:	....
Interlocutor:	Thank you.

Part 2   (4 minutes)   *Magazine covers – Insurance company*

Interlocutor: Now, in this part of the test you're going to do something together. Here are some pictures which show people in different situations.

Place the picture sheet for Test 3 in front of the candidates.

First, I'd like you to look at pictures *and* (*Select from pictures A–F*) and talk together about what the people might be thinking.

You have about a minute for this, so don't worry if I interrupt you.

Candidates
A & B: [*One minute.*]

Interlocutor: Thank you. Now, look at all the pictures. I'd like you to imagine that an insurance company has decided to produce a magazine which will be circulated internally, inside the company.

Talk together about the way these pictures might reflect the work and image of the insurance company. Then decide which ones to choose for the front cover of the first and second editions of this company magazine.

You have about three minutes to talk about this.

Candidates
A & B: [*Three minutes.*]

Interlocutor: Thank you. *Retrieve picture sheet.*

Part 3   (12 minutes)   *Teaching and learning*

Interlocutor: Now, in this part of the test you're going to talk on your own for about two minutes. You need to listen while your partner is speaking because you'll be asked to comment afterwards.

So, (*Candidate A*), I'm going to give you a card with a question written on it and I'd like you to tell us what you think. There are also some ideas on the card for you to use if you like.

All right? Here is your card, and a copy for you, (*Candidate B*).

Hand over a copy of prompt card 3a to each candidate.

Remember, (*Candidate A*), you have about two minutes to talk before we join in.

[*Allow up to 10 seconds before saying, if necessary*: Would you like to begin now?]

Candidate A: [*Two minutes.*]

Interlocutor: Thank you.

*Select **one** appropriate follow-up question for Candidate B.*

- What do you think?
- Is there anything you would like to add?
- Is there anything you don't agree with?
- How does this differ from your experience?

Candidate B: [*One minute.*]

Interlocutor: *Address **one** of the following questions to both candidates.*

- What makes learning difficult?
- Who decides what we learn at school?
- What rewards can you get from studying?

Candidates
A & B: [*One minute.*]

Interlocutor: Thank you. *Retrieve cards.*

Now, (*Candidate B*), it's your turn to be given a question.

Hand over a copy of prompt card 3b to both candidates.

Here is your card, and a copy for you, (*Candidate A*). Remember, (*Candidate B*), you have about two minutes to tell us what you think, and there are some ideas on the card for you to use if you like. All right?

[*Allow up to 10 seconds before saying, if necessary*: Would you like to begin now?]

Candidate B: [*Two minutes.*]

Interlocutor: Thank you.

*Select **one** appropriate follow-up question for Candidate A.*

- What do you think?
- Is there anything you would like to add?
- Is there anything you don't agree with?
- How does this differ from your experience?

Candidate A: [*One minute.*]

Interlocutor: *Address **one** of the following questions to both candidates.*

- What is the status of teachers in your country?
- How can teachers make learning a more enjoyable experience?
- Do you think you would make a good teacher?

Candidates
A & B: [*One minute.*]

Interlocutor: Thank you. *Retrieve cards.*

Interlocutor: Now, to finish the test, we're going to talk about teaching and learning in general.

Address a selection of the following questions to both candidates.

- Why do we forget things we have learnt?
- How important is it when you're learning, to have a sense of curiosity?
- Thinking about computers, how have they changed ways of teaching and learning?
- Do you think everyone should go to university?
- What sort of environment do you find suits you best for studying?
- Some people say that knowledge is power. Why do you think that is?

Candidates
A & B: [*Four minutes.*]

Interlocutor: Thank you. That is the end of the test.

Test 4

Note: In the examination, there will be both an Assessor and an Interlocutor in the room.

The visual material for Part 2 is on pages C8 and C9 in the colour section of the Student's Book. The prompt cards for Part 3 are on pages C10 to C12 in the colour section of the Student's Book.

This test is also suitable for groups of three students.

Part 1   (3 minutes, or 4 minutes for groups of three)

Interlocutor:	Good morning/afternoon. My name is .... and this is my colleague .... And your names are .... ?
Candidates:	....
Interlocutor:	Thank you. Could I have your mark sheets, please?
	Now, first of all, it would be nice to find out something about each of you.
	Where are you from, (*Candidate A*)? And you, (*Candidate B*)? [And you, (*Candidate C*)?]
	Select a further question for each candidate.

- What are you doing at the moment?
- Do you enjoy your work / your studies?
- What's the best thing about the area that you come from?
- How much longer do you think you'll be studying English?
- Do you know what job you'd like to be doing in 5 years' time?

Candidates A, B [& C]:	....
Interlocutor:	*Select a further question for each candidate.*

- Do you think your education is/was good preparation for the world of work?
- Can you tell us something about where you're living now? What, if anything, would you like to change about it?
- Could you tell us if there's a particular time of year you especially like?
- What about your hobbies? What's your main interest?
- Are there any sports that you're good at?
- What about food? If you eat out, what kind of restaurants do you prefer?

Candidates A, B [& C]:	....
Interlocutor:	Thank you. Now, we'd like to ask you what you think about one or two things.

*Select **one** more question for each candidate.*

- How well can you learn a language without living in the country concerned?
- Thinking about yourself, how representative are you of someone from your country?
- Thinking about computers, how important do you think they are in schools nowadays?
- How important is the place or environment where you study?
- How do you think your chosen area of work will change in the future?
- Do you feel optimistic about the future? Why?

Candidates A, B [& C]:	....
Interlocutor:	Thank you.

Part 2	(4 minutes, or 6 minutes for groups of three)	*Nature magazine – Importance of water*

Interlocutor:	Now, in this part of the test you're going to do something together. Here are some pictures which show water. *Place the picture sheet for Test 4 in front of the candidates.* First, I'd like you to look at pictures *and* (*Select from pictures A–E*) and talk together about the mood the photographer wanted to portray. You have about a minute (*two minutes*) for this, so don't worry if I interrupt you.
Candidates A, B [& C]:	[*One minute, or two minutes for groups of three.*]
Interlocutor:	Thank you. Now, look at all the pictures. I'd like you to imagine that a nature magazine is publishing a special edition on the part water plays in our lives. Talk together about how these pictures illustrate the importance of water. Then decide what other aspects, not shown here, should be included in this special edition. You have about three minutes (*four minutes*) to talk about this.
Candidates A, B [& C]:	[*Three minutes, or four minutes for groups of three.*]
Interlocutor:	Thank you. *Retrieve picture sheet.*

Part 3 (12 minutes, or 18 minutes for groups of three)   *Communicating*

Interlocutor: Now, in this part of the test you're going to talk on your own for about two minutes. You need to listen while your partner is speaking because you'll be asked to comment afterwards.

So, (*Candidate A*), I'm going to give you a card with a question written on it and I'd like you to tell us what you think. There are also some ideas on the card for you to use if you like.

All right? Here is your card, and a copy for you, (*Candidate B [and Candidate C]*).

Hand over a copy of prompt card 4a to each candidate.

Remember, (*Candidate A*), you have about two minutes to talk before we join in.

[*Allow up to 10 seconds before saying, if necessary:* Would you like to begin now?]

Candidate A: [*Two minutes.*]

Interlocutor: Thank you.

*Select **one** appropriate follow-up question for Candidate B.*

- What do you think?
- Is there anything you would like to add?
- Is there anything you don't agree with?
- How does this differ from your experience?

Candidate B: [*One minute.*]

Interlocutor: *Address **one** of the following questions to both (all three) candidates.*

- What kind of things are difficult to express in a foreign language?
- How good were/are your teachers at communicating their enthusiasm?
- Would you rather express your ideas in writing or in speech?

Candidates
A, B [& C]: [*One minute.*]

Interlocutor: Thank you. *Retrieve cards.*

Now, (*Candidate B*), it's your turn to be given a question.

Hand over a copy of prompt card 4b to each candidate.

Here is your card, and a copy for you, (*Candidate A [and Candidate C]*). Remember, (*Candidate B*), you have about two minutes to tell us what you think, and there are some ideas on the card for you to use if you like. All right?

[*Allow up to 10 seconds before saying, if necessary*: Would you like to begin now?]

Candidate B: [*Two minutes.*]

Interlocutor: Thank you.

Select **one** *appropriate follow-up question for Candidate A [or C].*

- What do you think?
- Is there anything you would like to add?
- Is there anything you don't agree with?
- How does this differ from your experience?

Candidate A [or C]: [*One minute.*]

Interlocutor: *Address* **one** *of the following questions to both (all three) candidates.*

- When might it be better to write letters by hand?
- Do you think the on-street public phone has a future?
- Does technology lead to unnecessary communication? (How?)

Candidates A, B [& C]: [*One minute.*]

Interlocutor: Thank you. *Retrieve cards.*

Now, (*Candidate C*), it's your turn to be given a question.

Hand over a copy of prompt card 4c to each candidate.

Here is your card, and a copy for you, (*Candidate A [and Candidate B]*). Remember, (*Candidate C*), you have about two minutes to tell us what you think, and there are some ideas on the card for you to use if you like. All right?

[*Allow up to 10 seconds before saying, if necessary*: Would you like to begin now?]

Candidate C: [*Two minutes.*]

Interlocutor: Thank you.

Select **one** *appropriate follow-up question for Candidate A.*

- What do you think?
- Is there anything you would like to add?
- Is there anything you don't agree with?
- How does this differ from your experience?

Candidate A: [*One minute.*]

Interlocutor: *Address* **one** *of the following questions to both (all three) candidates.*

- Does TV have a negative effect on conversation?
- Do you think newspapers and magazines have a future?
- How influenced are you by advertisements?

Candidates A, B [& C]:	[*One minute.*]
Interlocutor:	Thank you. *Retrieve cards.*

Interlocutor:	Now, to finish the test, we're going to talk about communicating in general.

Address a selection of the following questions to both (all three) candidates.

- Which is more difficult – to be a good speaker or a good listener?
- What can music communicate that other media can't?
- Some people say that modern art doesn't communicate anything to them. What do you think?
- Do you think handwriting can communicate anything about an individual?
- How important is body language in your culture?
- What does the way we dress say about us?
- Does learning about different cultures help us to communicate more effectively?
- What do you feel about the continuing growth of English as an international language?

Candidates A, B [& C]:	[*Four minutes, or six minutes for groups of three.*]
Interlocutor:	Thank you. That is the end of the test.

Test 1 Key

Paper 1 Reading (1 hour 30 minutes)

Part 1 (one mark for each correct answer)

1 B   2 A   3 D   4 A   5 C   6 B   7 B   8 A   9 D
10 C   11 D   12 A   13 A   14 C   15 B   16 A
17 D   18 A

Part 2 (two marks for each correct answer)

19 B   20 C   21 C   22 D   23 C   24 D   25 C   26 B

Part 3 (two marks for each correct answer)

27 G   28 B   29 F   30 E   31 D   32 C   33 A

Part 4 (two marks for each correct answer)

34 B   35 A   36 D   37 C   38 B   39 A   40 C

Paper 2 Writing (2 hours)

Task-specific mark schemes

Question 1: Escape to the country

Content
Major points:
Discussion of   – problems of city life
                – advantages of country life
                – problems of country life

Further points:
Any points relevant to the area of discussion.

Range
Language for expressing and supporting opinions.

Appropriacy of register and format
Register appropriate to an article for a magazine. Article may make use of headings.

Organisation and cohesion
Clear development of arguments and ideas. Adequate use of linking and paragraphing.

Target reader
Would understand the writer's viewpoint.

Question 2: *Launching a new soft drink*
Content
Description and discussion of the different methods for advertising the soft drink, with reference to the ideas provided, and explanation as to why the writer's ideas are particularly effective.

Range
Language for describing, analysing, explaining and making recommendations.

Appropriacy of register and format
Register and format appropriate for that of a proposal – could make use of relevant section headings. Register can be formal or neutral in tone, but must be consistent.

Organisation and cohesion
Presentation of ideas and information should be well-structured. Adequate use of linking and paragraphing.

Target reader
The company would have a clear idea of what is being recommended.

Question 3: *International Festival of Drama Review*
Content
Review of the drama festival and comment on what they learned from the experience.

Range
Language of description, analysis and evaluation.

Appropriacy of register and format
Register and format should be appropriate for a review in a school/college magazine. Register can be formal/informal, but must be consistent.

Organisation and cohesion
Clear development of points. Adequate use of paragraphing and linking.

Target reader
Would be informed about the drama festival and what the writer learned from the experience.

Question 4: *College handbook for new students*
Content
Letter should give information about the college and the social organisations, and make new students feel welcome.

Range
Language for giving information.

Appropriacy of register and format
Informal/neutral, but must be consistent.
Should be encouraging and lively in tone, friendly and welcoming.

Organisation and cohesion
Well-organised, possibly with sub-headings.

Target reader
Would be well-informed about what is available at the college.

Question 5(a): The Accidental Tourist
Content
Clear reference to the book chosen.
Brief summary of the book leading to an analysis of the funny and sad elements in the story.

Range
Language of description, narration and evaluation.

Appropriacy of register and format
Review with register and format appropriate to a student magazine. Register must be consistent throughout.

Organisation and cohesion
Clear development from introduction to development of the main focus, leading to a clear conclusion.

Target reader
Would be informed about the book and appreciate both the funny and sad elements of the story.

Question 5(b): The Day of the Triffids
Content
Clear reference to the book chosen.
Description of the triffids and what they do, and discussion of their impact on society.

Range
Language of description, narration, analysis and evaluation.

Appropriacy of register and format
Neutral composition.

Organisation and cohesion
Clear presentation and development of ideas. Appropriate paragraphing and linking. Clear conclusion.

Target reader
Would be informed about the triffids and understand their role in the book.

Question 5(c): Our Man in Havana
Content
Close reference to the book chosen.
Clear focus on whether or not Wormold achieves the status of a hero.

Range
Language of description, narration and evaluation.

Appropriacy of register and format
Formal register, and format consistent and appropriate for a letter to a literary magazine.

Organisation and cohesion
Clear presentation and development of ideas, with appropriate linking and paragraphing. Clear conclusion.

Target reader
Would have a clear idea of the writer's viewpoint with regard to whether or not Wormold achieves the status of a hero.

Paper 3   Use of English (1 hour 30 minutes)

Part 1   (one mark for each correct answer)

1 back   2 part   3 it   4 there   5 against / to   6 little
7 brought   8 until / till   9 that   10 to   11 went
12 would / could / might   13 means   14 hardly / scarcely
15 so / as / that

Part 2   (one mark for each correct answer)

16 invariably   17 pressure   18 excessive   19 essential
20 retailers   21 centrally   22 illogical   23 unavoidable
24 criticism(s)   25 efficiency

Part 3   (two marks for each correct answer)

26 matter   27 flat   28 fell   29 beat   30 led   31 press

Part 4   (one mark for each correct section)

32 no (previous) time (before) (1) + has the present government (ever) (1)
33 is / seems to be (rather / somewhat) lacking (in) (1) + clarity / cohesion (1)
34 not to (1) + take sides (1)
35 to meet (1) + anyone / anybody / someone / somebody (who is) more generous than OR + a more generous person than (1)
36 reveal / manifest / show / display / demonstrate / have the slightest hesitation in OR hesitate in the slightest (1)
   + when it came to OR before / about (1)
37 (had) never crossed (1) + my mind (1)
38 (the reason) why Liz (should have) left / departed (1) + (so) suddenly (1)
39 had (finally) run (1) + out of (1)

Part 5   (questions 40–43 two marks for each correct answer)

40 analogy of market place particularly appropriate in a business text

41 they are arrived at by chance or are a reflection of the personality of the person in charge of the company
42 their personal goals coincide with company goals so they can work on both at the same time
43 workers are not permitted to develop and implement their own ideas for improvement, thus restricting company development
   no group vision
44 (one mark for each content point, up to ten marks for summary skills)
   The paragraph should include the following points:
   i   both need to be in good shape / have level of fitness
   ii require mental determination to succeed
   iii perform better as a team
   iv need to raise the level of objectives when they are approached so that progress continues to be made / reassess their goals continually

Paper 4   Listening (40 minutes approximately)

Part 1   (one mark for each correct answer)
1 A   2 B   3 B   4 B   5 C   6 A   7 A   8 B

Part 2   (one mark for each correct answer)
9 transporting goods   10 (welcome) shelter   11 copper
12 ice(-)dance / ice(-)dancing   13 air(-)conditioning / air conditioners
14 spray   15 logo(s)   16 20 / twenty hours   17 fog

Part 3   (one mark for each correct answer)
18 B   19 C   20 A   21 D   22 C

Part 4   (one mark for each correct answer)
23 B   24 A   25 A   26 C   27 B   28 C

Transcript   *Certificate of Proficiency in English Listening Test. Test 1.*

I'm going to give you the instructions for this test.

I'll introduce each part of the test and give you time to look at the questions.

At the start of each piece you'll hear this sound:

tone

You'll hear each piece twice.

Remember, while you're listening, write your answers on the question paper.

You'll have five minutes at the end of the test to copy your answers onto the separate answer sheet.

There will now be a pause. You must ask any questions now, because you must not speak during the test.

[pause]

PART 1

Now open your question paper and look at Part One.

[pause]

You'll hear four different extracts. For questions 1 to 8, choose the answer (A, B or C) which fits best according to what you hear. There are two questions for each extract.

Extract 1

[pause]

tone

Presenter: Do you *have* to do all these interviews to publicise the film, Tom? Is it in your contract?

Actor: No, but I feel it's part of my responsibility to advertise it. Having done a few low-budget films that come out for a week and then disappear, it's really disappointing. So you go on and do the local radio so that people come and see it, especially if it's something that you're proud of. I think you often find that if an actor isn't prepared to do an interview, it's more often than not because they're not happy with themselves or the product.

Presenter: Sometimes with the big stars there's this long list of things we're not allowed to ask them about!

Actor: That's not fair, is it? If they say they're going to do the interview, then they should. If you were to ask me an incredibly awkward question, I could just say, 'Well, I don't want to talk about that'. But as I say, I'm here to plug the film! I mean, I'm not here to make myself a big celebrity or anything. That's what . . .

[pause]

tone

[The recording is repeated.]

[pause]

Extract 2

[pause]

tone

How would you describe your personality? Anxious? Outgoing? The list could be quite long. In fact, psychologists have found approaching 18,000 words to describe personality. If so much of our language is given over to this activity, then the description of personality must be an important part of everyday life. But perhaps we are influenced in the way we judge another's character by our general liking or disliking for them. A beloved uncle is eccentric, whereas a more unpopular one is mad. So clearly there are advantages to the scientific study of personality.

   As one interesting example of what's been discovered, take extroversion and introversion. Extroversion means being very outward-looking, sociable, noisy, and introversion is the opposite. Originally, it was thought that people fell into one or other of these two groups. But now all studies of personality show that they are not separate categories, but represent the two extremes of a continuum, and that in fact most people are somewhere in the middle.

[pause]

tone

[The recording is repeated.]

[pause]

Extract 3 [pause]

tone

When I think of my childhood home now, it seems that its beauty is protected by its remoteness and that very remoteness made me want not so much to leave, but escape. The corner of Scotland I come from is a peninsula cut off from the rest of Scotland by the sea and the stark emptiness of the moors.

Last summer I went home and tried insanely to buy a house. I'd been nurturing this idea for some time. The moment I set eyes on the house, I knew it was for me, as though the hand of destiny had guided me down the track.

What was I thinking? – I had no livelihood there. I was a foreign correspondent whose only specialism was international affairs. My 'home' and everything I knew best was in London. The house was built of granite and seemed to grow organically from the rock, as though it was part of the natural topography. It was timeless, unchanging, predictable and certain, just what I was seeking. I made an offer on it, which wasn't accepted. I was saved from my own sentimental folly.

[pause]

tone

[The recording is repeated.]

[pause]

Extract 4 [pause]

tone

Interviewer: So, why did you decide to write this book on the USA **now**?
Author: Well a few years ago, when I was there, I was asked to write a book about it; and I must have spent at least four or five minutes contemplating this exercise. The States is more like a world than a country; you could as well write a book about people, or about life. There's so much material – it's all embracing. Then, years later, as I was emptying out my desk drawers to gather together a selection of past pieces I'd written, I found that I'd already written a book about the US, but it was unpremeditated, accidental, and in instalments. Of the hundreds of thousands of words I seem to have written for newspapers and magazines in the last fifteen years, about half of them seem to be about the US. But I hope these disparate pieces add up to something. I know you can approach the subject only if you come at it from at least a dozen different directions.

[pause]

tone

[The recording is repeated.]

That's the end of Part One.

Now turn to Part Two.

PART 2   [pause]

You will hear part of a radio programme about ice-skating rinks. For questions 9 to 17, complete the sentences with a word or short phrase.

You now have forty-five seconds in which to look at Part Two.

[pause]

tone

If you've ever been to watch any of Britain's professional ice-hockey teams, you've no doubt thrilled at the speed and agility of great athletes skating on indoor ice. But you've probably taken for granted the surface that makes it all possible. Nevertheless, the temperature and other characteristics of the surface can make the difference between a championship-winning performance and an embarrassing spill. Indoor ice rinks are used for all sorts of sports and recreational activities, in all of which the quality of the ice makes a big difference.

Ice-skating began as a means of transporting goods on the frozen rivers and canals throughout northern Europe long before anyone ever saw it as the recreational activity which it later became. Considering that skating for pleasure was done outdoors in the freezing winter weather, it's fair to say that indoor ice rinks were created because in those conditions they provided welcome shelter for those who enjoyed skating. It was only when ice became available year-round that sports such as hockey and skating had a chance to flourish.

In 1876 the first indoor rink opened in London, although the idea was not replicated up and down the country as had been predicted, as the process entailed making the ice by pumping a mixture of glycerine and water through copper pipes, a material which was expensive at that time. The first Olympic figure-skating competition was held on a refrigerated indoor rink as part of the Summer Games in London in 1908, though it was not until 1976 that ice-dancing, that is, interpreting music on skates, became a Winter Olympics sport. In the early twentieth century, electric refrigeration and indoor rinks made ice-skating popular everywhere.

The technology that makes indoor rinks possible is also found in refrigerators and air conditioning in our homes. In an indoor ice rink, the refrigerant doesn't cool the ice directly, as home systems do. Instead, it cools salt water that is pumped through an intricate system of pipes underneath the ice.

Laying down a good skating surface isn't as simple as making a tray of ice cubes. Freezing a rink correctly takes no less than a dozen stages, with some stages laying ice that is wafer thin. And what's best for one sport may be completely unacceptable for another! It takes up to seventy thousand litres of water to make a rink. The first two layers of ice, which are less than one millimetre thick, are applied via a spray to create a fine mist of water. The first layer freezes almost immediately after it's sprayed on, and then the second is applied. The second frozen layer is painted white, allowing for a strong contrast, for example, in hockey, between the black disc known as the puck and the ice. The third layer acts as a sealer for the paint. This layer then requires painting to create decorative backgrounds and, in the case of hockey, provide clear markings and display sponsors' logos. Once all the markings have dried, the final layer is gradually applied. This uses forty thousand litres of water which must be put on slowly with a hose at a rate of two to three thousand litres per hour. That means at least 15, at most 20 hours for this final layer. The less water is put on the floor at one time, the better the ice will be.

Brand new ice is called green ice because it hasn't been broken in yet. When creating a new rink, indoor conditions are very important, with the skating surface kept at –4.5 to –3° Celsius, the building temperature at about 17° Celsius, and the indoor humidity at about 30%. But if it's warm outdoors, the temperature has to be re-adjusted accordingly. Even one degree can make a big difference in the quality of the ice. In addition, a fog over the ice can be created by high humidity indoors which, of course, would hold a hockey game up.

So, on a hot summer's day when you…

[pause]

Now you'll hear Part Two again.

tone

[The recording is repeated.]

[pause]

That's the end of Part Two.

Now turn to Part Three.

[pause]

PART 3   *You will hear the beginning of a radio interview with Stephen Perrins, a composer of musicals. For questions 18 to 22, choose the answer (A, B, C or D) which fits best according to what you hear.*

You now have one minute in which to look at Part Three.

[pause]

tone

Interviewer:	My guest today started out in the world of serious music and showed great promise as an avant garde composer, but he made the surprising leap into the world of the musical theatre. Welcome, Stephen Perrins.
Stephen Perrins:	Thank you.
Interviewer:	Stephen, what made you change from serious music to musicals?
Stephen Perrins:	Well, my parents were both professors of music, so I dutifully went to music college, studied composition, and wrote rather inaccessible music. But I suppose really my heart's always been in the theatre, and I soon found myself writing songs in secret, drawing my inspiration from musicals.
Interviewer:	Did you try to get them published?

Stephen Perrins:	No, for a long time I kept them to myself, even though I thought they were commercial. I suppose I had something of an inferiority complex about them, because they were a bit slushy, and I was sure my family and college would think they were below me.
Interviewer:	So what happened?
Stephen Perrins:	Well, we had a very light-hearted end-of-year show at college, and I decided, more or less on impulse, to sing one of my songs, because it happened to fit rather neatly into a sketch that Jenny Fisher and I wrote, which was a spoof opera. And it kind of stole the show. A year later a schoolteacher friend, who'd been in the cast, got in touch with me – he wanted a short musical for a concert at his school. In fact, just as an experiment, Jenny and I had already worked up the opera sketch into something we renamed *Goldringer*, without any real idea of what to do with it next, so it just needed a bit of tinkering.
Interviewer:	That was lucky.
Stephen Perrins:	The real break was that the music critic of a national paper had a child at the school, and the following Sunday we read this rave review saying that Jenny and I were the future of the musical, and of course we were on cloud nine, and we immediately had music publishers lining up.
Interviewer:	How did your family react?
Stephen Perrins:	Oh, they were aghast at first, but they came round, and they've been right behind us ever since.
Interviewer:	You've always said you won't do the lyrics of your songs. I presume you've tried.
Stephen Perrins:	I did with my early songs. In fact I could knock them off with a rather suspect facility. But I realised that if I wrote both the words and the music I'd be working in a kind of vacuum, and what I enjoy most is the collaboration and sparking off each other's ideas.
Interviewer:	There was a story in the papers recently that you wanted to direct your musicals, too. Has anything come of that?
Stephen Perrins:	No, that just wasn't true. I never claim to be a director, I always think when you've actually appointed the director for a show, you shouldn't undermine them. For example, in one of my shows, which Helen Downes directed, I wasn't that happy with the design, but she was passionate to have it, and it was right not to interfere.
Interviewer:	Now in the last few years you've had great international success, but for some of the more upmarket newspapers, it seems, you simply can't put a foot right.
Stephen Perrins:	No, and I don't really know quite why. Maybe I'm being big-headed, but I don't think it's because of the music. I think it's more that I'm not really that bothered about my image, so I don't do masses of PR. Which means I leave myself open to that carping sort of criticism.
Interviewer:	It seems to me it's a kind of distaste for the popularity of your music.
Stephen Perrins:	It's like the time when serious art critics looked down on the late 19th-century artists, and their paintings were considered worthless. The fact is that if you went into an art gallery, guess where the public were.
Interviewer:	Just as the public are always to be found at your musicals. Stephen Perrins, thank you.
Stephen Perrins:	Thank you.

[pause]

Now you'll hear Part Three again.

tone

[The recording is repeated.]

[pause]

That's the end of Part Three.

Now turn to Part Four.

PART 4   [pause]

You will hear part of a radio arts programme, in which two people, Arthur and Carla, are discussing a book called Windworld. *For questions 23 to 28, decide whether the opinions are expressed by only one of the speakers, or whether the speakers agree. Write A for Arthur, C for Carla, or B for both, where they agree.*

You now have thirty seconds in which to look at Part Four.

[pause]

tone

Presenter:	Today on *A Good Read* we are talking about George Swallow's novel *Windworld*, published last year and it has just won the Bateman Prize. We have with us Arthur Lachman, writer, and Carla Fletcher, who lectures in Engineering at King's College. Arthur, let's start with you…
Arthur:	Well, I read the novel when it first came out and I was very happy to be asked to re-read it for this programme and I remembered the powerful characterisation – the certainty of touch – particularly of the older protagonist, Joe Bean, and his sisters, in the throes of change from one era to another.
Carla:	Rather miserable characters but assured portraits.
Arthur:	Mmmm… What I valued as well was the atmosphere Swallow creates, the sense that everything he created felt right within the time and place. Did you find that?
Carla:	Very interesting question. As a scientist, I always come to books with a critical eye for technical details. As I say, Joe Bean and his family as *people* rang incredibly true for me. I found myself doubting whether certain incidents, ummm… certain assumptions squared with the period in which the book is set.
Arthur:	I have to say that I found the sheer amount of technical detail about inventions, which Swallow included as a labour of love, I have no doubt, gave the lay person a hard time, making it difficult to follow the plot.
Carla:	Umm. I actually found myself comparing all these descriptions of the windmills and pumps with… with his earlier works *Learner Games* and *Thorn*… which both dealt with the same period but neither of which included this kind of complexity. Much more populist… deliberately more accessible to a wide readership.
Arthur:	There is much to *link* the writing of all three books: you can recognise Swallow's individual voice in all of them – he's speaking to one specific audience in my view.
Presenter:	Do you feel *Windworld* is a great novel?
Arthur:	Oh very much so. The current of the author's own life in the East of England pulses through the whole work so compellingly. So, yes, I would say that it lifts this book… ummm… into the category of great writing.

Carla: I wouldn't be quite that positive, though I do agree that the character of Joe Bean draws its strength from the writer's close acquaintance with Joe's environment: to my mind he's almost certainly Swallow putting himself in another age – positioning himself, with his upbringing and his character and his beliefs, in the 18th century.

Arthur: I was intrigued by some of these set episodes, like the incident with the birds. It was genuinely fascinating, I thought. I understand the film rights have been bought. Do you think it'll work as well as the book does?

Carla: No question – if they keep away from too much social realism and misery. If they don't make Joe's story the central one, it'll die a death.

Arthur: Well – just about all the stories are likely to come through well, in my opinion. We'll have to see how it turns out!

[pause]

Now you'll hear Part Four again.

tone

[The recording is repeated.]

[pause]

That's the end of Part Four.

There will now be a pause of five minutes for you to copy your answers onto the separate answer sheet. Be sure to follow the numbering of all the questions. I'll remind you when there is one minute left, so that you're sure to finish in time.

[pause]

You have one more minute left.

[pause]

That's the end of the test. Please stop now. Your supervisor will now collect all the question papers and answer sheets.

Test 2 Key

Paper 1   Reading (1 hour 30 minutes)

Part 1   (one mark for each correct answer)

1 B   2 C   3 A   4 D   5 A   6 B   7 B   8 D   9 A
10 B   11 C   12 A   13 B   14 A   15 C   16 A
17 C   18 A

Part 2   (two marks for each correct answer)

19 A   20 D   21 C   22 D   23 A   24 D   25 B   26 A

Part 3   (two marks for each correct answer)

27 B   28 H   29 G   30 E   31 A   32 F   33 C

Part 4   (two marks for each correct answer)

34 D   35 B   36 A   37 C   38 A   39 D   40 C

Paper 2   Writing (2 hours)

Task-specific mark schemes

Question 1: Growing old

Content
Major points:
Discussion of: – whether or not old people have something useful to offer society
                – whether or not other people have to look after old people
                – the advantages and disadvantages that belong to old age

Further points:
Relevant examples to support either or both of the views expressed.

Range
Language for expressing and supporting opinions, and for expressing agreement and disagreement.

Appropriacy of register and format
Formal/semi-formal letter format. Register appropriate to the writer's role as reader of a magazine writing in to express opinions.

Organisation and cohesion
Clear organisation of points. Adequate use of paragraphing and linking.

Target reader
Would understand the writer's viewpoint.

Question 2: Differences between rich and poor

Content
There may be some brief introduction to the causes of poverty, but the main content should be suggestions on ways of helping to reduce the differences between rich and poor, plus comments on why these ideas might work.

Range
Language for describing, analysing, evaluating and making recommendations.

Appropriacy of register and format
Register and format appropriate for that of a proposal – could make use of relevant section headings. Register can be formal or neutral in tone, but must be consistent.

Organisation and cohesion
Presentation of ideas and information should be well-structured. Adequate use of linking and paragraphing.

Target reader
The reader would have a clear idea of what suggestions are being made.

Question 3: New leisure centre, library or playground?

Content
Description and analysis of what local residents think about the three proposals, including recommendations based on the opinions that local residents have expressed.

Range
Language of description, analysis and recommendation.

Appropriacy of register and format
Register and format appropriate for a report for the local council – could make use of section headings. Register must be consistent.

Organisation and cohesion
Clear organisation of content with adequate use of linking and paragraphing.

Target reader
The local council would have a clear idea of what the local residents think the money should be spent on.

Question 4: 'A Country of Contrasts'

Content
Description of the different types of places that can be found.
Opinions about these different places.
Opinion of how these contrasts make the country an interesting place to visit.

Range
Language of description, comparison and opinion.

Appropriacy of register and format
Appropriate to an article in a travel magazine.

Organisation and cohesion
Magazine-style article possibly with headings to introduce different places.

Target reader
Would want to visit the country because of the contrasts and have a clear idea of what the contrasts were.

Question 5(a): The Accidental Tourist

Content
Clear reference to the book chosen.
Evaluation of the statement and whether or not it is true.

Range
Language of description, narration and evaluation.

Appropriacy of register and format
Neutral essay.

Organisation and cohesion
Clear presentation and development of ideas. Appropriate paragraphing and linking. Clear conclusion.

Target reader
Would understand the viewpoint of the writer with regard to Macon.

Question 5(b): The Day of the Triffids

Content
Clear reference to the book chosen.
Description of events that changed the world, and an evaluation of whether or not the book gives an optimistic view of human nature.

Range
Language of description, narration and evaluation.

Appropriacy of register and format
Review with register and format appropriate for a literary magazine. Register must be consistent throughout.

Organisation and cohesion
Clear development from introduction to development of the main focus, leading to a clear conclusion.

Target reader
Would have a clear understanding of the writer's viewpoint.

Question 5(c): Our Man in Havana

Content
Close reference to the book chosen. Evaluation of whether the statement is true or not. Reference to what is amusing and entertaining in the book, and whether or not it has a serious moral purpose. Both parts of the question need to be addressed.

Range
Language of description, narration and evaluation.

Appropriacy of register and format
Clear presentation and development of ideas. Appropriate paragraphing and linking. The two parts of the question can be dealt with separately or together. Clear conclusion.

Organisation and cohesion
Neutral essay.

Target reader
Would understand the viewpoint of the writer.

Paper 3　Use of English (1 hour 30 minutes)

Part 1　(one mark for each correct answer)

1 one / that　　**2** only NOT just　　**3** how　　**4** other　　**5** should
6 from　　**7** such　　**8** with　　**9** not　　**10** regard / respect / reference
NOT answers　　**11** none / nothing　　**12** far　　**13** however
14 may / might / would　　**15** though / as

Part 2　(one mark for each correct answer)

16 regularity　　**17** justice　　**18** mathematicians　　**19** repeatedly
20 unravel　　**21** breakthroughs　　**22** meteorology　　**23** spectacular
24 awesome　　**25** disclose

Part 3　(two marks for each correct answer)

26 short　　**27** rough　　**28** covered　　**29** touched　　**30** track
31 question

Part 4　(one mark for each correct section)

32 as I enjoy / like reading, (1) + there are times when / that OR at times (1)
33 had been published / was published (1) + did the president make (1)
34 been for your support (1) + I'd still be (1)
35 expressed / voiced / made clear (1) + (their) disapproval of / about (1)
36 as no surprise to me (1) + to hear about / of (1)
37 ought to / should / had / 'd better say / mention (1) + anything / a word about (1)
38 (completely / totally) at a (total / complete) loss (1) + to explain / understand / know / account for (the reason) as to / over (the reason) (1)
39 Minister's resignation (1) + resulted from (1)

Part 5   (questions 40–43 two marks for each correct answer)

40 his wife gets angry and his children are contemptuous / mocking / insult him
41 they cannot be stopped
42 they are (self-sufficient) loners
43 more facilities would avoid overcrowding and therefore increase enjoyment
44 (one mark for each content point, up to ten marks for summary skills)
    The paragraph should include the following points:
    i   the need to be alone / get away from others
    ii personal challenge
    iii the pleasure of being in the fresh air
    iv the need for stimulation / uplift / curiosity brought by new scenes and activities

Paper 4   Listening (40 minutes approximately)

Part 1   (one mark for each correct answer)
1 B   2 A   3 C   4 A   5 C   6 B   7 C   8 A

Part 2   (one mark for each correct answer)
9 zoology   10 (human) eye(s)   11 feathers
12 bee   13 rescuers / rescue(-)teams   14 (a) low speed / low speeds
15 energy source / battery   16 take(-)off / taking off   17 (the) noise

Part 3   (one mark for each correct answer)
18 B   19 A   20 B   21 C   22 A

Part 4   (one mark for each correct answer)
23 G   24 M   25 B   26 B   27 G   28 M

Transcript   *Certificate of Proficiency in English Listening Test. Test 2.*

I'm going to give you the instructions for this test.

I'll introduce each part of the test and give you time to look at the questions.

At the start of each piece you'll hear this sound:

tone

You'll hear each piece twice.

Remember, while you're listening, write your answers on the question paper.

You'll have five minutes at the end of the test to copy your answers onto the separate answer sheet.

There will now be a pause. You must ask any questions now, because you must not speak during the test.

[pause]

Now open your question paper and look at Part One.

[pause]

PART 1 *You'll hear four different extracts. For questions 1 to 8, choose the answer (A, B or C) which fits best according to what you hear. There are two questions for each extract.*

Extract 1 [pause]

tone

Interviewer: So, finally Nigel, you achieved your ambition and made the break into films. It seems to me you got a lot of stick about it, I mean, on the one hand from jealous film makers, which is understandable, but also, more interestingly, from the literary community in Ireland, who seemed to be upset that you were doing something quite so vulgar. Although presumably it's good for the way Ireland is perceived abroad.

Nigel: That's perfectly true. But you know, at the time, novelists didn't make films. Now it's quite a common thing.

Interviewer: But isn't it that rather conservative, orthodox Irish thing that serious writers don't stray away from the high realm of literature?

Nigel: I wouldn't call it conservative and orthodox. I would say actually that the importance of writing in Irish culture is huge. It's always been the subversive force in the culture itself.

Interviewer: But conservative in the sense that you're not allowed to do anything else if that's what you're capable of doing.

Nigel: Well, it's kind of seen as a vocation in a way, I suppose.

[pause]

tone

[The recording is repeated.]

[pause]

Extract 2 [pause]

tone

Woman: Do you know, an amazing thing happened to me yesterday: two totally unconnected people looked me straight in the eye and told me they were sorry!

Man: No!

Woman: Honest! You know I have a permit to park outside my flat?

Man: Yes?

Woman: Well I was sent a new one in January, but some idiot had written the wrong year on it, and I was fined for parking illegally.

Man: Oh no!

Woman: So I went storming into the town hall, spluttering with rage. And would you believe, the woman behind the desk not only said sorry, but owned up that she recognised her writing. It really took the wind out of my sails, and I found myself clucking sympathetically and saying what an easy mistake it was to make! Then in the afternoon I had someone coming round to repair my cooker, and he turned up three hours late. I went ballistic when he arrived, but he apologised for disrupting my day, and I stopped frothing at the mouth. Then his company rang, and it turned out it wasn't even his fault, so of course I felt I'd made a real fool of myself!

[pause]

tone

[The recording is repeated.]

[pause]

Extract 3   [pause]

tone

Have you ever wondered why something makes you laugh? Human beings love to laugh so much that there are actually industries built around laughter. For us it seems so natural, but laughter is a distinctly human response. Philosopher John Morreall believes that the first human laughter may have begun as a gesture of shared relief at the passing of danger. The relaxation that results from a bout of laughter inhibits the biological fight-or-flight response, laughter may signal trust in one's companions. Studies have also found that dominant individuals – whether boss, tribal chief or family patriarch – use humour more than their subordinates. If you've often thought that people at work laugh sycophantically when the boss laughs, you're very perceptive. In such cases, Morreall says, controlling the laughter of a group becomes a way of exercising power by controlling the group dynamics. So laughter, like much human behaviour, must have evolved to influence the way people interact. And there have been numerous interesting...

[pause]

tone

[The recording is repeated.]

[pause]

Extract 4   [pause]

tone

One day in 1993 I got a call from TV producer Tim Taylor, asking me to meet him to discuss a new series popularising history. I'd never heard of Tim but he explained historian Mike Lewis was the other person fronting the programme. I'd met Mike before and couldn't think of anyone I'd rather embark on a project with. We met and, though I had some reservations about the way it would all turn out, I agreed to sign up for the pilot programme, hoping that the TV company would like this initial episode.

Now the problem with a pilot is that everyone knows best – until it's finished you can't tell who's right. We weren't confident that history alone would galvanise an audience. My experience of storytelling might prove useful in getting history across. I thought this was a great idea and got really engrossed in my solo about a fanatical medieval monk. Looking back, this does look terribly self-indulgent and reduces the programme to a snail's crawl. But we submitted it to the broadcasters who were critical of this, but they offered us a series and the rest is history – quite literally!

[pause]

tone

[The recording is repeated.]

[pause]

That's the end of Part One.

Now turn to Part Two.

[pause]

PART 2   *You will hear an engineer giving a talk on the radio about future developments in robot design. For questions 9 to 17, complete the sentences with a word or short phrase.*

You now have forty-five seconds in which to look at Part Two.

[pause]

tone

By dint of brute force and massive use of external energy we can outpace all other animals, but when it comes to sheer finesse and the use of cunning tricks of aerodynamics, the animal kingdom leaves us standing. Increasingly, engineers are looking to zoology for clues on improving performance or making robots that can cope with harsh environments. But although it takes modern science to fathom exactly how animals do things, there's nothing new about the basic principle of trying to copy nature. For instance would we have tried so hard to create flying machines if it wasn't for the example of birds? But in the early days of aeronautical engineering, scientists had inadequate observation techniques, they relied solely on the human eye. Initially, as a consequence of that, they thought that the secret of how birds flew lay in the flapping movements that they made and the pattern of feathers alone. If they'd looked at the *right* aspects of engineering and bird flight, they would have achieved powered flight and manned flight earlier.

Interestingly, flapping wings are now making a comeback. After a century in which powered flight used only fixed and rotating wings, engineers are rediscovering the benefits of how insects fly. They're trying to produce a fifteen-centimetre flying robot, derived in part from the bee. The potential uses of such a machine are limited only by the imagination. For example, it could be used where buildings have collapsed and there are possible casualties to be rescued. If a person is trapped and is still breathing, then there is an opening through which air is coming in and a robot could fly in through this opening and take a photograph which would help the rescuers to assess the position and plan the operation better.

But why model the robot on insect flight at all? The answer to this is that only an insect is up to the demands of the job. If you think of working inside buildings, manoeuvring at low speeds is essential because otherwise the robot will collide with obstructions. It will need to be able to hover, because if it finds something of interest, it will have to stay still to take a clear picture of it. And finally, and this is a very important requirement, the robot must fly in a power-efficient way, because it will be fairly small so there won't be much space to put in an energy source. So the first thought of the design team was to use some conventional design like a fixed-wing forward thrust, as in the usual plane, or alternatively, rotary wings, found in a helicopter, and scale them down to fifteen centimetres. The problem is that planes require considerable speed to achieve take-off, so they can't fly very slowly and also they can't hover or manoeuvre in a very agile way. So would helicopters be more appropriate? They can certainly fly very slowly and hover and they are very manoeuvrable, but they have other problems: they generate considerable noise, so that would rule out any situations where the robots would need to remain undetected such as in undercover surveillance or data gathering projects. So, having eliminated the tried and tested designs, the question was what other proven design was there? In 300 million years flapping-wing insects have certainly proved their efficiency. They offer agility even at low speed, they can do amazing aerobatics, they can hover, and unlike helicopters their flight mechanism generates very little noise.

There's more to insect flight than just flapping wings though. The movements of those wings are remarkably complex. For engineers to create a successful flying robot they will have to draw on the accumulated knowledge of zoologists. It's going to be a hard but fascinating journey of discovery.

[pause]

Now you'll hear Part Two again.

tone

[The recording is repeated.]

[pause]

That's the end of Part Two.

Now turn to Part Three.

[pause]

PART 3   *You will hear a radio interview with a music critic, Hazel Fisher, about some classical music awards. For questions 18 to 22, choose the answer (A, B, C or D) which fits best according to what you hear.*

You now have one minute in which to look at Part Three.

[pause]

tone

Presenter:	Now here's our regular critic Hazel Fisher, who's been invited to vote in a new initiative, the Classical Music Awards. Hazel, giving awards for classical music is surely a healthy development, isn't it?
Hazel:	On the face of it, yes. When these awards were announced recently, it seemed like a genuinely enlightened idea. There's the prospect of a huge amount of publicity surrounding the event, so it seemed like a high-profile boost for the serious classical market.
Presenter:	And it's well-timed, too, isn't it?
Hazel:	Very well-timed, because a lot of people don't hold out much hope for classical music sales. Here at last, I thought, would be recognition for all those small record companies who continue to produce worthwhile releases, while the major companies are just concerned with a safe repertoire and endlessly reissuing their old recordings. And at the same time, it would help all those performers who produce excellent music without any of the trappings of jetset celebrity. You know, it makes me so cross that the glossiest new recordings nowadays are usually turned into an international circus of the same bankable names. It certainly wouldn't come amiss if a wider range of performers were brought into the limelight for a change.
Presenter:	So why did your enthusiasm evaporate?
Hazel:	It was when the list of nominations was announced. It was clear that the whole exercise was nothing more than a cynical marketing exercise, with two aims. One was to eat even further into the distinction between what's worthwhile and what's just opportunistic rubbish. And the second was to bolster the sales of the industry's heavyweight companies, who have invested so heavily in these crossover products, that won't stand the test of time.
Presenter:	Crossover?
Hazel:	That's when classical singers, orchestras, and so on, play non-classical music, like musicals or pop or jazz.
Presenter:	Right. Now, you also object to the way the final choices are going to be made, don't you?
Hazel:	Yes, I do. Ten nominations've been made in each category, and the winners will be chosen by an 'academy' of recording industry stalwarts. So if there's no bias there, I will eat my hat. It hasn't been made public how the voting will work, but rumour has it that it's pretty opaque, though designed to be as fair as possible. Goodness knows how long the whole thing will take, especially as there are a lot of sections, but that's their problem. They've allowed several months before the awards ceremony.
Presenter:	And what do you think about the nominations themselves?
Hazel:	I find those absolutely mind-boggling. It's still a mystery who actually compiled these shortlists, but they would have us believe that film music and other lightweight work are among the ten best 'classical' albums of the year. And the fact that they only include one or two genuine classical items in each list shows what they're really interested in. For instance, take the Male Artist of the Year category: it's beyond me how anyone can choose between, say, a singer specialising in 17th and 18th century operas and a composer of film scores. It would take a more sophisticated knowledge of the musical world than I have.
Presenter:	So what's your verdict?

Hazel: Well, it's hard to escape the conclusion that the organising group, and the record companies that constitute it, are happy to move the goalposts whenever it suits them commercially. Which brings up a wonderful irony too. Recently the record companies have been complaining bitterly because a CD of popular classics given a synthesiser makeover was included in the classical bestsellers chart. But now they seem only too happy to go along with this farrago, which does more to confuse the boundaries between what's classical and what's popular (if that's the right classification) than any amount of synthesiser doodlings.

Presenter: But do you think we should even care about it at all?

[pause]

Now you'll hear Part Three again.

tone

[The recording is repeated.]

[pause]

That's the end of Part Three.

Now turn to Part Four.

[pause]

PART 4   *You will hear two neighbours, Graham and Melinda, discussing changes that the town council are making to a public park near their homes. For questions 23 to 28, decide whether the opinions are expressed by only one of the speakers, or whether the speakers agree. Write G from Graham, M for Melinda, or B for both, where they agree.*

You now have thirty seconds in which to look at Part Four.

[pause]

tone

Graham: Have you seen what's happening in Baxton Park, Melinda? The town council's put all this fencing round so you can't get in. And they've brought in an earthmover to churn up all the grass and level the ground. It looks awful!

Melinda: Oh I know. It *is* a pity. It used to belong to some member of the aristocracy, you know, as part of her land, about a hundred years ago.

Graham: Yes, I think I heard that somewhere.

Melinda: Apparently she gave it to the people of Baxton for their 'recreational use'. That's what she said in her will.

Graham: Oh did she? But then surely they can't go ahead with developing it? She can't have wanted it dug up like this! It's against the terms of the will!

Melinda: I suppose it depends what you mean by 'recreational use', doesn't it? It could mean for sport, couldn't it? And we know they're going to put two football pitches and a cricket ground on it.

Graham: Yes, *and* what they call a hospitality building right in the middle. That's being paid for by one of the local companies, you know.

Melinda: Oh dear! I can just see it being used to host parties every weekend, and then people'll be coming and going at all hours of the night! How are we ever going to get a decent night's sleep?

Graham: Oh, I think the trees will probably muffle the sound quite a bit, after all they're quite dense round here. I'm more worried about the parking. This is going to attract a lot of people and the road's busy enough as it is.

Melinda: I know, I often have difficulty finding a space. I mean it took me a quarter of an hour the other day. What really gets me is the way all this has been managed. It's so underhand! I mean, we scotched the plan when it surfaced five years ago, and now, without a word of warning to any of us locals, it's reared its ugly head again.

Graham: We really should have been given the chance to have our say, shouldn't we? That's the least you'd expect. You know, I was just wondering...

Melinda: What? Go on.

Graham: Well, of course, it's just a suspicion, I haven't any proof as such, but I was just wondering if anybody on the council had been, you know, got at by the developers. I mean, it's quite a big project. There'll be some lucrative contracts in there.

Melinda: You're getting paranoid, Graham! Been watching too many movies about big business! No, I think we just have to accept it. There's nothing any of us can do about it.

Graham: What about calling a protest meeting? We could phone up the local paper and get their photographer round. You never know, we might just get them to think again.

Melinda: Oh yes? And do you really think that's going to get us anywhere?

Graham: Well OK, just a thought.

Melinda: Maybe we should try looking on the bright side…

[pause]

Now you'll hear Part Four again.

tone

[The recording is repeated.]

[pause]

That's the end of Part Four.

There will now be a pause of five minutes for you to copy your answers onto the separate answer sheet. Be sure to follow the numbering of all the questions. I'll remind you when there is one minute left, so that you're sure to finish in time.

[pause]

You have one more minute left.

[pause]

That's the end of the test. Please stop now. Your supervisor will now collect all the question papers and answer sheets.

Test 3 Key

Paper 1   Reading (1 hour 30 minutes)

Part 1   (one mark for each correct answer)
1 A   2 B   3 B   4 A   5 C   6 D   7 A   8 B   9 A
10 C   11 B   12 D   13 D   14 C   15 B   16 A
17 C   18 D

Part 2   (two marks for each correct answer)
19 C   20 A   21 B   22 A   23 B   24 D   25 B   26 D

Part 3   (two marks for each correct answer)
27 G   28 E   29 B   30 H   31 D   32 A   33 C

Part 4   (two marks for each correct answer)
34 A   35 C   36 C   37 D   38 B   39 C   40 B

Paper 2   Writing (2 hours)

Task-specific mark schemes

Question 1: Employment in the future
Content
Major points:
Discussion of: – whether or not unemployment will continue to rise as a result of
    the increasing use of machines/computers and the need for profits
  – whether or not new developments will create new job
    opportunities
  – the writer's own viewpoint on the matter

Range
Language for expressing and supporting opinions, and for reaching conclusions.

Appropriacy of register and format
Formal essay-type register.
Register appropriate to the writer's role as a student.

Organisation and cohesion
Clear organisation of points. Adequate use of linking and paragraphing
Logical development of argument and clear conclusion(s).

Target reader
The tutor would understand the writer's viewpoint.

Question 2: 'Healthy Lifestyles for the Young' magazine

Content
Should discuss possible coverage of health and lifestyle issues, and ideas for interesting content for young people.
Organisation of different types of articles, presentation, style.

Range
Language for describing.
Language for analysing.
Language for hypothesising and recommending.

Appropriacy of register and format
Proposal format – may make use of clear section headings.
Register appropriate to semi-formal relationship.

Organisation and cohesion
Well-structured sections.
Clear presentation of ideas.
Clear linking and paragraphing.

Target reader
Would understand what the writer is proposing.

Question 3: *Protecting endangered animals, birds and plants*

Content
Description of why forms of nature and wild life are endangered, and concrete suggestions for helping to protect them.

Range
Language of description, analysis and suggestion.

Appropriacy of register and format
Register and format appropriate for a letter to a magazine. Register must be consistent.

Organisation and cohesion
Early reference to reason for writing. Clear organisation of points. Adequate use of linking and paragraphing.

Target reader
Readers would have a clear idea of the writer's suggestions for saving endangered species.

Question 4: 'Good Neighbours'

Content
Description of a difficult situation.
How the neighbour helped out.
Conclusions about what makes a good neighbour.

Range
Language of description and narration.

Appropriacy of register and format
Register appropriate for a popular magazine.
Article format could lend itself to headings.

Organisation and cohesion
Clear development of description and narration.
Adequate use of linking and paragraphing.

Target reader
Would be interested in reading the story of the event, understand why the
neighbour was so appreciated by the writer and what, in the opinion of the writer,
makes a good neighbour.

Question 5(a): The Accidental Tourist

Content
Clear reference to the book chosen.
Description and analysis of reasons for the failure of the marriage of Sarah and
Macon. Evaluation of whether Macon's comment is true or not.

Range
Language of description, narration and evaluation.

Appropriacy of register and format
Neutral article.

Organisation and cohesion
Clear presentation and development of ideas. Appropriate linking and
paragraphing. Clear conclusion.

Target reader
Would understand the viewpoint of the writer and have a clear idea of the reasons
for the failure of the marriage of Sarah and Macon.

Question 5(b): The Day of the Triffids

Content
Clear reference to the book chosen.
Evaluation of whether the statement is true or not.
Description of what the triffids are and what they do, and reference to other
characters and how they respond to the situation.

Range
Language of description, narration, comparison and evaluation.

Appropriacy of register and format
Formal letter appropriate for a literary magazine. Register must be consistent
throughout.

Organisation and cohesion
Clear presentation and development of ideas with appropriate linking of
paragraphs from the introduction to the main body of the letter. Clear conclusion.

Target reader
Would be clear about the writer's viewpoint on the matter.

Question 5(c): Our Man in Havana
Content
Close reference to the book chosen.
Description of the portrayal of Wormold as a secret agent, and an analysis of how far the novel is a typical spy story.

Range
Language of description, narration, analysis and evaluation.

Appropriacy of register and format
Review with register and format appropriate to the Arts Section of a newspaper. Register must be consistent throughout.

Organisation and cohesion
Clear presentation and development of ideas. Appropriate paragraphing and linking. Clear conclusion.

Target reader
Would be informed about the book and the portrayal of Wormold as a secret agent, and how far the novel is a typical spy story.

Paper 3   Use of English (1 hour 30 minutes)

Part 1   (one mark for each correct answer)
1 who   2 to   3 when   4 having   5 of   6 due / thanks / owing
7 what   8 its / the   9 no   10 it   11 into   12 only
13 whose   14 because / as / since   15 could / may / might

Part 2   (one mark for each correct answer)
16 infancy   17 institutions   18 exclusively   19 insight
20 disappearing   21 commitment   22 inaccessible   23 loneliness
24 immersion   25 undeniably

Part 3   (two marks for each correct answer)
26 reflection   27 bear   28 stage   29 line   30 volume   31 moved

Part 4   (one mark for each correct section)
32 were (completely) taken (1) + aback (completely) at / by (1)
33 given (1) + a standing ovation (1)
34 matter (1) + how late it (1)
35 no idea (of) what (1) + was going (1)
36 (many) hours (have passed) since OR(many) hours ago that (1) + I (first) joined (1)
37 any / a likelihood / possibility / chance (1) + of (my / me) having a (private / quiet) (1)
38 look / are (remarkably / very / incredibly) alike (1) + in the (1)
39 do / can we account for (1) + the fact that the / the way (that) the / why the (1)

Part 5 (questions 40–43 two marks for each correct answer)

40 They process the information according to their experience and needs.
41 By seeing them regularly many times.
42 (They're like a net) – they filter information / data from the outside world / they prevent certain things / information / data from passing through.
43 Instinctively but with cultural differences
44 (one mark for each content point, up to ten marks for summary skills)
    The paragraph should include the following points:
      i seeing parts rather than the whole – flecks of colour / notes
     ii not being able to distinguish objects
   iii too much noise to pick out sounds
   iv it would put our lives in danger

Paper 4   Listening (40 minutes approximately)

Part 1 (one mark for each correct answer)
1 B   **2** C   **3** B   **4** C   **5** C   **6** A   **7** C   **8** B

Part 2 (one mark for each correct answer)
9 rattle   **10** cliff faces/cliffs   **11** window(-)sills   **12** repopulate
13 cover   **14** nesting   **15** a/one hundred/100   **16** (deliberate) neglect/
being neglected (deliberately)   **17** locations

Part 3 (one mark for each correct answer)
18 B   **19** C   **20** A   **21** D   **22** D

Part 4 (one mark for each correct answer)
23 T   **24** B   **25** C   **26** C   **27** T   **28** T

Transcript   *Certificate of Proficiency in English Listening Test. Test 3.*

I'm going to give you the instructions for this test.

I'll introduce each part of the test and give you time to look at the questions.

At the start of each piece you'll hear this sound:

tone

You'll hear each piece twice.

Remember, while you're listening, write your answers on the question paper.

You'll have five minutes at the end of the test to copy your answers onto the separate answer sheet.

There will now be a pause. You must ask any questions now, because you must not speak during the test.

[pause]

Now open your question paper and look at Part One.

[pause]

PART 1 *You'll hear four different extracts. For questions 1 to 8, choose the answer (A, B or C) which fits best according to what you hear. There are two questions for each extract.*

Extract 1 [pause]

tone

Interviewer: Reading your book about your career exploits, I have to say it does sound to me as if you've done what a lot of kids dream of, and managed to make a living out of, let's face it, larks, high spirits. It's akin to having the nerve to go to a company and ask for a million pounds to go on holiday.

Balloonist: It's been wonderful.

Interviewer: Long before this you started as a photographer.

Balloonist: Yes, I've always liked imagery – that's part of the reason why I got involved in all these dreams, as you call them, of adventure. It's pure theatre, really.

Interviewer: And you did a spell in advertising, I read.

Balloonist: Yes, I did … and it was at that time in 1975 when I had my first balloon flight and in those days they really were the stuff of dreams, and it occurred to me that there must be a possibility to do something here with these huge billboards in the sky and to make a living out of it.

[pause]

tone

[The recording is repeated.]

[pause]

Extract 2 [pause]

tone

Presenter: Robin Adams, you've recently published a book of photographs of famous women, with the proceeds going to a number of charities. How did you decide who to photograph? Are they people you had an interest in already because they're very high profile? Or did you think, there's a hook there? And I'm actually interested in photographing this person.

Robin Adams:	Well, although they are all, as you say, high-profile women, we went about this in a low-key way. I'd heard of most of them, or, at least, their reputations, and had seen their various media images. There's always more to people than meets the eye, or the camera lens – and it was that something I wanted to expose. But this proved more of a thorny issue than I'd expected.
Presenter:	Oh really, I thought it would have been easier, they would have known exactly how to present themselves. They've done it so many times before.
Robin Adams:	Well, in my work, I get behind the veneer of the face. The women feel secure enough to open up about themselves, and I have to be careful not to betray too much of that.

[pause]

tone

[The recording is repeated.]

[pause]

Extract 3 [pause]

tone

I'm ringing about Stoke City football team. I've been a supporter of theirs for years. You'll have noticed in Saturday's match just how much we miss Steve Harris. We lack the power up front since he's gone. There were some nice touches from Evans, but the real strength that Harris represented, that's served us well over the years, was just missing on Saturday. It was a gaping hole in Stoke's attack, and I'm sure the manager's regretting selling him. I mean, we don't need the £11 million that Barcelona paid us, we need our goal-scorer back! If you speak to the Stoke fans, most of them will say no amount of training will produce another Harris. He provided the punch and that just wasn't there on Saturday. No wonder we lost! Still, for a good thirty minutes our lads dominated the field. They showed some spirit, I must say. They haven't thrown in the towel yet, so provided we get a good replacement for Harris, (and the manager'd better get it right this time!) maybe there'll be light at the end of the tunnel after all.

[pause]

tone

[The recording is repeated.]

[pause]

Extract 4 [pause]

tone

When we managed to get it hoisted, for the first time since 1800, well, it was a struggle, but thank goodness, we did it. So then this immense amount of sail was hanging in the museum. I thought people would come in and go Wow! and then read the relevant information boards we'd put underneath. But there was a new dimension to this exhibition that I simply hadn't envisaged. People felt as if they were travelling back in time, because here they could see for themselves the reality of damage to a sailing ship on the high seas two centuries ago. You can see this great rent, which is about eight metres deep in the centre, and as you go closer to the cloth, not only do you get this sort of shine on the cloth itself, and you can see how it's aged and coloured, but at various points there are gunpowder stains of shots that must have passed through it, so again there's the reality. This isn't just a textbook or a computer game about history for you to look at, this is the…

[pause]

tone

[The recording is repeated.]

[pause]

That's the end of Part One.

Now turn to Part Two.

[pause]

PART 2   *You will hear a short talk about a bird of prey called the kestrel. For questions 9 to 17, complete the sentences with a word or short phrase.*

You now have forty-five seconds in which to look at Part Two.

[pause]

tone

Interviewer: Today we're very pleased to welcome Sean Pearce, from the British Nature Trust, who is going to talk about one of the most beautiful birds to be seen in Britain: the kestrel. Sean…

Sean Pearce: Thank you. I'm here to launch the Trust's publicity campaign. Recent, relatively small-scale research we've carried out is indicating a significant decline in kestrel numbers and basically we're asking the public to help us get our statistics even more accurate.

But first, let me give you a few facts on the bird to help in sighting and a little background information and an explanation of the cause of some of its problems. The kestrel – its unusual name comes from the old French for a rattle – and that refers not to the fluttering wing movement but to its cry. This is very distinctive. It has the capacity to hang in the air for long periods with its wings vibrating so rapidly you can hardly see the movement. This is a picture of a mature male hovering. Notice its beautiful plumage in different shades of brown and cream and its easily recognised fluted tail – the picture is reproduced for you in the survey material to help in identification.

Now, before the diversification of their habitat in the last hundred years or so, kestrels were solely to be found nesting on cliff faces and their main prey was the vole – a small mouse-like creature in the countryside but which now will be unfamiliar to many of you. But, *now*, kestrels are increasingly making their home in towns where they're not an uncommon sight these days, they settle on the window sills of houses, skyscrapers etc. Now, turning to food in this new habitat, they depend not on their rural staple of voles, who don't appear to do very well in this setting, but on whichever small rodents they can find, and these are to be found in abundance. Kestrels have also found a viable habitat in upland areas, mainly the preserve of sheep farming, which is proving to be a problem, as we shall see.

Kestrels have actually been known to be highly successful in keeping up their numbers over the years because of their notable ability to quickly repopulate. How this works is simple – they aren't dependent on one locale and can gradually move to where the habitat is more favourable. But this is only effective when problems affect a small area. Difficulties at a macro level are now beginning to affect them. For example, upland kestrels suffer due to increasing sheep densities. Their grazing decreases the vegetation which provides cover for the main upland kestrel food, the vole, which of course, in turn means a large population of the birds of prey cannot be maintained. These problems have been compounded by long periods of heavy precipitation – mainly rain, but also snow, which causes nesting difficulties.

Now let's have a look at some of the population statistics. Excuse me, there are thought to be in the region of 50,000 breeding pairs – that's 100,000 adults – left in the UK, which means, with an average of three offspring per pair, circa 250,000 birds. But kestrels have a relatively low survival rate when young, which helps cushion extremes in population – a built-in control, if you like. Only a proportion survive – many succumbing in infancy because of their parents' deliberate neglect. Now, because of the changes mentioned earlier, the population is falling further and will soon, we believe, not be able to recover. Something *must* be done and that's where the public come in!

What we ask of you is to take two or three of these sighting forms, I'll pass some out in a moment, but I'll also leave a pile at the back, which you can fill in when you have a sighting. They ask for information about numbers, timing and, *crucially*, location. There is a picture, as promised, and simple diagrammatic information to help you establish whether what you have seen is really a kestrel and not confuse it with, for example, a peregrine falcon.

Thank you very much indeed for your time and attention. I hope you'll be able to help us.

[pause]

Now you'll hear Part Two again.

tone

[The recording is repeated.]

[pause]

That's the end of Part Two.

Now turn to Part Three.

[pause]

PART 3   *You will hear the historian, George Davies, talking about society and the theatre in England in the time of William Shakespeare. For questions 18 to 22, choose the answer (A, B, C or D) which fits best according to what you hear.*

You now have one minute in which to look at Part Three.

[pause]

tone

Interviewer: We welcome today Professor George Davies from the University of Wales. Professor Davies is an expert on society in sixteenth-century England, the time of Queen Elizabeth the First and, of course, Shakespeare. So how would you categorise society at that time, Professor?

Professor: Well, it was certainly a society undergoing dramatic changes in which there was an explosion of interest in the language, even though the printed word hadn't become universally available. We don't quite know exactly how many people could read and write but literacy would not have extended to all levels of society. Some historians call it an illiterate society, but that seems rather pejorative. No, the best way of putting it, in my view, is to refer to it as a *pre*-literate society, like most societies that have ever been on the planet. In fact our society, in which we tend to expect everybody to be literate, is the one which is out of step.

Interviewer: So how did this pre-literacy affect ability to communicate at that time?

Professor: What it meant was that the prime form of communication was direct speech, face to face, which means communication involving the body, the stance, the distance between people. It also meant that people were much more finely tuned to the spoken word, they could take in more of it, they could listen in a more acute way. It's therefore quite natural that the art form which corresponds to that particular situation should be drama.

Interviewer: One thing that has always puzzled me is where did the actors in the sixteenth century learn their craft? Were there any drama schools then?

Professor: Well, Shakespeare's actors, the boys and the older men in his company, didn't actually have any acting training before they joined his company. You see, in Shakespeare's day you learned your school work by repeating it out loud all day long. The arts of oratory and rhetoric were part of your normal education and they were also the means by which you learned. So they had wonderful voice training, which enabled them to develop an individual style.

Interviewer: I've always thought of the Elizabethan society as one that revelled in its voice, that at its heart delighted in giving voice to words. Would that be correct?

Professor: I would certainly think that the atmosphere in the average theatre of the time would surprise us today. I believe it would sound and feel more like a present day football ground! In a modern theatre there's a sort of reverential hush as the darkness descends and we feel, you know, that we're in some sort of temple devoted to the worship of great art. But then, the atmosphere would have been much noisier. Remember Shakespeare and his contemporaries had theatres which were open to the sky, and so the noise of the city, the shouts of the street sellers, the neighing of horses and so forth would add to and mix with the sounds of the stage and indeed, in my view, would comment on them.

Interviewer: So, in the same way, this was not a world for the shy or the softly spoken?

Professor: Not at all. People's voices in the sixteenth century, it seems to me, wouldn't have been geared to the exchange of intimate revelations about the self. This is a notion of speaking that is a twentieth-century concept, as is our notion that a play should give you the intimate, personal feelings of the author or of a character on the stage. Then, art was largely about external issues, how a country should be governed, how one should deal with rebellion, questions of that order.

Interviewer: Fascinating, Professor. I'd like at this point to bring in another speaker who is going to tell us about Elizabethan court life and how Shakespeare…

[pause]

Now you'll hear Part Three again.

tone

[The recording is repeated.]

[pause]

That's the end of Part Three.

Now turn to Part Four.

[pause]

PART 4 *You will hear a conversation in which Clare and Tom, who teach English to foreign students at the same language school, discuss Tom's first week at the school. For questions 23 to 28, decide whether the opinions are expressed by only one of the speakers, or whether the speakers agree. Write C for Clare, T for Tom, or B for both, where they agree.*

You now have thirty seconds in which to look at Part Four.

[pause]

tone

Clare: Hello, Tom. How are you finding teaching here?

Tom: Bit early to say, really, Clare. But I get the odd feeling that somehow the school's successful despite itself.

Clare: How do you mean?

Tom: Well, it *claims* to be really up-to-date, but the buildings and furniture have seen better days, and the equipment's on its last legs, yet amazingly the students seem happy.

Clare: Maybe the good atmosphere is partly *because* the building and things aren't up to much. People don't feel they always have to be on their best behaviour.

Tom: That just sounds like an excuse for being an also-ran! These days you can't compete unless you can really provide the best. That's the trouble with these small family-owned schools. So many of the owners still seem to be in the Dark Ages.

Clare: In what way?

Tom: They seem to believe that if the teaching's good enough, they'll get students, but quality doesn't sell itself these days, if it ever did.

Clare: That's because most of the students come through word of mouth. Though I don't know how long that'll keep the school going. So many other schools have really *good* marketing machines. But I suppose we're going to have to bite the bullet. I doubt if there'll be a place much longer for family-owned schools, the way things are going, with so many being taken over by large companies that own several schools.

Tom: Do you think there's a chance of surviving if they find a niche?

Clare: Like English for business, or for university, you mean?

Tom: Yes.

Clare:	That's a point. There are some very successful ones that have stayed one-offs.
Tom:	Well, their days are numbered if you ask me. More and more are being bought by companies.
Clare:	Yes. Some companies seem to offer a whole range of subjects, not just English.
Tom:	I think that's good, because they can bring together a mixture of teachers of different subjects.
Clare:	That's all very well, but it doesn't do much for your professional development, does it?
Tom:	Surely it gives a different perspective on the classroom? A geography teacher, say, might give you fresh ideas that you can apply in teaching English or maths.
Clare:	I've always found it a real eye-opener talking to other English teachers. Because people's approaches to teaching the same subject can vary so much. I sometimes feel I'm not on the same wavelength as science teachers!
Tom:	Oh Clare, honestly!
Clare:	Well maybe I'm exaggerating a bit, but you know what I mean.
Tom:	Actually I sometimes feel that about classes, you know? And I feel it's my role as the teacher to make sure we get on all right, but I can't always do it.
Clare:	Surely it depends on the class too? Each class develops its own culture, and you may not be able to do anything about it. You just have to accept that you don't get on with every class.
Tom:	I reckon that's a bit of a cop-out, really. I'm sure you ought to be flexible enough to deal with any class effectively, but I can't always do it.
Clare:	Maybe it comes with experience. Do you think you'll stay here long?
Tom:	Depends how it pans out. I need to believe I'm doing something worthwhile, even if the money isn't brilliant. I hope that comes, when I've had a chance to get settled.
Clare:	It doesn't matter that much to me, I suppose, because I put a lot of energy into other things. So I could put up with quite a lot, as long as I've got enough to live on, of course.
Tom:	Mm. I wish I had the time for other things. I'm sure…

[pause]

Now you'll hear Part Four again.

tone

[The recording is repeated.]

[pause]

That's the end of Part Four.

There will now be a pause of five minutes for you to copy your answers onto the separate answer sheet. Be sure to follow the numbering of all the questions. I'll remind you when there is one minute left, so that you're sure to finish in time.

[pause]

You have one more minute left.

[pause]

That's the end of the test. Please stop now. Your supervisor will now collect all the question papers and answer sheets.

Test 4 Key

Paper 1   Reading (1 hour 30 minutes)

Part 1   (one mark for each correct answer)

1 A	2 C	3 B	4 D	5 B	6 A	7 A	8 C	9 A
10 B	11 D	12 C	13 C	14 B	15 A	16 D		
17 C	18 D							

Part 2   (two marks for each correct answer)

19 C	20 D	21 B	22 A	23 B	24 A	25 C	26 A

Part 3   (two marks for each correct answer)

27 E	28 C	29 H	30 B	31 G	32 A	33 D

Part 4   (two marks for each correct answer)

34 B	35 B	36 D	37 B	38 C	39 C	40 A

Paper 2   Writing (2 hours)

Task-specific mark schemes

Question 1: Fast food restaurant

Content
Major points:
Discussion of: The advantages versus the drawbacks, e.g.
– encouraging more people to visit the town
– the possible increase in revenue
– the interest generated in local history

Range
Language for expressing and supporting views, and for making recommendations.

Appropriacy of register and format
Appropriate format for a proposal – may make use of headings.

Organisation and cohesion
Ideas organised and well-structured.
Adequate use of paragraphing and linking.

Target reader
The local council would understand the writer's viewpoint.

Question 2: *Review of an adventure holiday*

Content
Description of the adventure holiday, with reference to exploring interesting places, meeting different people and experiencing a different lifestyle, as well as some kind of recommendation, relevant to students wanting a cheap but exciting holiday.

Range
Language of description, narration, evaluation and recommendation.

Appropriacy of register and format
Formal/informal register appropriate for a review in a college magazine. Register must be consistent throughout.

Organisation and cohesion
Clear development of ideas with adequate use of linking and paragraphing, and possible use of headings.

Target reader
Would be informed about the holiday.
Would be able to decide whether or not it was a holiday they would want to experience.

Question 3: *Improving education in your country*

Content
Description of present provision of education, with an analysis and evaluation of areas that could be improved, followed by concrete suggestions for bringing about improvement.

Range
Language of description, analysis, suggestion and recommendation.

Appropriacy of register and format
Register and format appropriate for a proposal – may make use of section headings.
Register must be consistent throughout.

Organisation and cohesion
Clear organisation of content with adequate use of linking and paragraphing.

Target reader
The Minister would have a clear understanding of the ideas put forward.

Question 4: *'I've always wanted to learn how to...'*

Content
Description of the particular skill the writer wants to acquire, plus an explanation of what is attractive about this skill. Description of what the writer would do with this skill.

Range
Language of description.

Appropriacy of register and format
Register and format appropriate for a magazine article. Possible use of section headings.

Organisation and cohesion
Ideas clearly organised. Adequate use of paragraphing and linking.

Target reader
Would have a clear idea of what skill the writer wanted to learn and what they would do with it.

Question 5(a): The Accidental Tourist

Content
Clear reference to the book chosen.
Recommendation of the book leading to emphasis on portrayal of Alexander and his relationship with his mother, Muriel, and with Macon.

Range
Language of description, narration and recommendation. Some language of description and narration relating to the characters in question and their relationships.

Appropriacy of register and format
Formal letter.

Organisation and cohesion
Clear presentation and development of ideas with appropriate linking of paragraphs from the introduction to the main body of the letter and the conclusion.

Target reader
Would know whether the novel would be suitable for the proposed exhibition.

Question 5(b): The Day of the Triffids

Content
Clear reference to the book chosen.
Description of the dramatic events in the story, and a description of the impact on the characters.

Range
Language of description and narration.

Appropriacy of register and format
Consistent and appropriate style for that of a report.

Organisation and cohesion
Clear presentation and development of ideas, with appropriate linking and paragraphing. May make use of section headings. Clear conclusion.

Target reader
Would be informed about the events and characters in the novel.

Question 5(c): Our Man in Havana

Content
Close reference to the book chosen.
Reference to how the relationship develops over the three visits Wormold makes to Dr Hasselbacher's flat.

Range
Language of description, narration and evaluation.

Appropriacy of register and format
Register appropriate to an article for a literary magazine.

Organisation and cohesion
Clear presentation and development of ideas. The account of the three visits can be dealt with together or separately. Appropriate linking and paragraphing required. Clear conclusion.

Target reader
Would have a clear idea of the characters of Wormold and Dr Hasselbacher, and how their relationship develops.

Paper 3 Use of English (1 hour 30 minutes)

Part 1   (one mark for each correct answer)

1 to	**2** its	**3** giving / considering	**4** but / yet / (al)though	**5** more
6 put	**7** Despite	**8** with	**9** into	**10** addition
11 should	**12** as	**13** not	**14** one	**15** far

Part 2   (one mark for each correct answer)

16 technological   **17** anxieties   **18** unquestionably   **19** assumption
20 destructive   **21** overwhelmingly   **22** beings   **23** pessimistically
24 imperfections   **25** heights

Part 3   (two marks for each correct answer)

26 cleared   **27** state   **28** set   **29** remain   **30** claimed   **31** fall

Part 4   (one mark for each correct section)

32 being driven by Paul's son (1) + at the time (1)
33 it not been for Nick's advice (1) + I would / I'd (1)
34 no point / time / stage (1) + did the police (actually) (ever) accuse (1)
35 much / a lot / a great deal to choose (1) + between (either of) (1)
36 is a total ban (1) + on (you / your) smoking (1)
37 makes (1) + no difference to Jenny (1)
38 improvement (1) + in the way the football team played / performed (1)
39 singled out the school library (1) + for criticism (1)

Part 5 (questions 40–43 two marks for each correct answer)

40 doom-mongers
41 the way in which old jobs are replaced by a greater number of new jobs because of changes in technology
42 innovations
43 Bill seems to be very interested in new technologies, so it's a surprise to find he uses something which is so old-fashioned
44 (one mark for each content point, up to ten marks for summary skills)
   The paragraph should include the following points:
   i technology doesn't necessarily lead to unemployment
   ii technology doesn't lead to low incomes
   iii new technologies don't completely replace old ones
   iv people sometimes prefer to keep old technologies

Paper 4   Listening (40 minutes approximately)

Part 1   (one mark for each correct answer)
1 C   2 B   3 B   4 A   5 C   6 A   7 B   8 A

Part 2   (one mark for each correct answer)
9 field training   10 tent   11 volcano (called Mount Erebus)
12 (flat (and) white) plain   13 roof (made out of lots of snow)
14 laboratories   15 month's salary   16 clothing / clothes (on display)
17 heroic failures

Part 3   (one mark for each correct answer)
18 B   19 A   20 D   21 C   22 C

Part 4   (one mark for each correct answer)
23 B   24 B   25 M   26 M   27 B   28 F

Transcript   *Certificate of Proficiency in English Listening Test. Test 4.*

I'm going to give you the instructions for this test.

I'll introduce each part of the test and give you time to look at the questions.

At the start of each piece you'll hear this sound:

tone

You'll hear each piece twice.

Remember, while you're listening, write your answers on the question paper.

You'll have five minutes at the end of the test to copy your answers onto the separate answer sheet.

There will now be a pause. You must ask any questions now, because you must not speak during the test.

[pause]

Now open your question paper and look at Part One.

[pause]

PART 1

You'll hear four different extracts. For questions 1 to 8, choose the answer (A, B or C) which fits best according to what you hear. There are two questions for each extract.

Extract 1

[pause]

tone

And now to American composer Carl Ruggles, who is still, years after his death, a total enigma. He worked at an incredibly slow pace, discarded far more than he kept, and has left us barely enough works to fill two CDs. Ruggles by name and rugged by nature, he was truly a man of the great outdoors. And he was never one to mince his words when commenting on his fellow musicians. He said of the French composer Debussy, 'There's nothing wrong with him that two weeks in the open air wouldn't cure!' and of the great romantic German composer Brahms, 'Why does he always hide behind all those musical devices? Why doesn't he come out and show us he's a man?' Here now is an orchestral piece of his, called 'Men and Angels.' It has a chequered history, as Ruggles originally wrote it in 1920 and then destroyed parts of it, so it was later revised. It is played here by members of the...

[pause]

tone

[The recording is repeated.]

[pause]

Extract 2

[pause]

tone

... it's a French novel, a worthy first novel, and I was fascinated with this because it's about the friendship between two women, something which isn't often written about, and also two very different women. The narrator is in her thirties with two children, and she writes for a living and needs a babysitter. The girl she winds up with, who comes to her through various friends, could not be more different. So it's a novel about differences; the girl, who is seen to be feckless and lacking in any sense of duty, and the narrator, who is bound up in her work to the exclusion of virtually everything else. Although that leads you to the question of the nature, I mean, what *is* work?

The themes I really enjoyed but, unfortunately, I don't think the translation works – I can't get any sense of the women's social context – I felt they were locked in a beautiful white cube somewhere and that, if only I understood where they were, I might have a better handle on them. I feel the translator was too concerned with putting his own stamp on the work.

[pause]

tone

[The recording is repeated.]

[pause]

Extract 3 [pause]

tone

Sociologically speaking, bags are an interesting feature of modern society. How we carry them is important. They're carried in the hand, on the crook of the arm, over the shoulder, on the back, in the form of pockets. Bags in fact are a way of keeping and displaying connections between our front and other parts of us, less visible, more vulnerable. A recent trend on the High Street was for girls to wear exquisitely functionless little rucksacks in the middle of their backs.

We often carry our cash, credit cards and other valuables in bags of one form or another, so they *can* show wealth and buying power. However, they also symbolise poverty and redundancy. The expression 'to give someone the sack' probably dates from 17th century France. In those days workmen provided their own tools and carried them in a bag, *sac* in French, which they took away with them upon leaving. So the word *sack* evolved from referring to the container for the workman's prized possessions, to the associated action of leaving a job, with the emphasis on *unwilling* departure.

[pause]

tone

[The recording is repeated.]

[pause]

Extract 4 [pause]

tone

Woman: You know I don't really enjoy going to the cinema anymore. I mean they spend millions now on making films and for what?

Man: Mmm, that level of expenditure seems to pay dividends. Cinema audiences have changed, and it looks to me as if most films just try to appeal to mass audiences.

Woman: Yes, they seem to make them to a format.

Man: It's 'oh, a disaster to overcome and then all live happily ever after'. Anything remotely sophisticated never makes it to the screen.

Woman: Well, they say cinema audiences have changed and it looks to me as if they're just trying to appeal to the lowest common denominator. Mind you, you still get a good cross-section going.

Man:	The ones I do enjoy are based on true-life stories. At least you feel you're seeing something real.
Woman:	Hmm... I'm not sure about that. They always twist the facts to make it more exciting I suppose.
Man:	Yeah, but I bet they do it because otherwise anybody in the story who is still around could see themselves really badly set up on screen – and would probably take them to court. *(laughs)*
Woman:	Yes... Anyway, real life is just much more mundane, isn't it?
Man:	Well, I don't think anyone would pay to see a film of my life.

[pause]

tone

[The recording is repeated.]

[pause]

That's the end of Part One.

Now turn to Part Two.

[pause]

PART 2   *You will hear a scientist talking about his first visit to the Antarctic. For questions 9 to 17, complete the sentences with a word or short phrase.*

You now have forty-five seconds in which to look at Part Two.

[pause]

tone

Presenter:	Dozens of scientists travel to the Antarctic every year to gather information on a range of subjects. Richard Hollingham is one of those scientists and he's here today to tell us about his first trip south and the survival course he and all other scientists have to go through when they arrive in the Antarctic.
Richard:	Well, the first day was spent getting accustomed to the sub-zero temperatures, which meant sliding down a glacier on our bottoms followed by a night sleeping out on the snow. This is what they call field training and anyone who has to spend significant periods of time working away from the main bases has to do it. And I really needed this training because on that first trip I was heading to an area of sea ice, where I would have to spend three months, in a tent! Can you imagine? This was going to be quite an experience.

Anyway, the setting for our first day's training was in the shadow of Mount Erebus, a volcano on the edge of the Ross Ice shelf. When I was there, a few wisps of sulphurous smoke rose from the summit of the crater. Behind us was a glacier and ahead a flat white plain which went all the way to the South Pole. The first day's training culminated in the construction of snow shelters. We were lucky with the weather. It was around minus ten and bright sun. There were twelve of us on this course and we split into teams and each team opted for a different type of shelter. The Canadians chose the igloo type, the New Zealanders the 'dig through a pile of snow' option and we went for a trench. We foolishly thought it would be the easiest. So we set to work and after a couple of hours, it was beautiful, it was deep and long but unfortunately far too wide. Everyone else had resounding success with their efforts but we were miserable failures. The idea was that what we'd dug should then be able to take a roof, but no matter how hard we tried, we couldn't get enough snow in blocks to bridge the gap. So in the end all we had was a long hole and that's how we came to sleep outside at night in one of the coldest places in the world.

This wasn't exactly the start we'd hoped for and we wistfully remembered what we'd seen of base camp at McMurdoch Sound; it was more like a town. Of course, there are the laboratories, but it's even got cable television. Society on base is fascinating. There's a black market in what at first seem very unlikely things. Things like newspapers and mineral water can change hands for considerable amounts of money; there's a rumour that salad greens, the most sought-after thing which are only occasionally shipped in, can fetch up to a month's salary for a dinner's worth.

The whole area around the base camp is full of reminders of some of the earliest explorers to that region; people like the British explorers, Shackleton and Scott. In fact, a few miles up the coast, the hut which Shackleton and Scott stayed in has still got the clothing they wore on display. Further on again, there's a base called the Scott Base and it's full of photographs of him, you know he lost his life on the return journey from the South Pole. The odd thing is there are no pictures of the man who actually got to the South Pole first, a Norwegian called Amundsen. I put this to a Norwegian on our survival course and he said Amundsen made it all look so easy whereas Scott had made it look much harder, the stuff of legends. So we carried on that British tradition of making things seem hard. Our training officer labelled us the 'heroic failures' because he'd never seen anybody get a shelter so wrong despite putting so much effort into it.

[pause]

Now you'll hear Part Two again.

tone

[The recording is repeated.]

[pause]

That's the end of Part Two.

Now turn to Part Three.

[pause]

PART 3 *You will hear part of a radio interview with a social worker. For questions 18 to 22, choose the answer (A, B, C or D) which fits best according to what you hear.*

You now have one minute in which to look at Part Three.

[pause]

tone

Presenter: In 1980 Tim Jarman left a comfortable university post for the insalubrious Northdown council estate, where housing is provided for the unemployed and those with low incomes. Here he set up a project to provide youth amenities. Tim, why did you give up your position at a university for a job on an estate?

Tim Jarman: Well, I was writing a book about social policy at the time, and I felt a bit of a hypocrite writing about poverty, telling people who work with the underprivileged what to do and not doing it myself. So I managed to get a grant from a charity, who helped me set up the Northdown Project.

Presenter: When you got there, you moved into a house, an old doctor's surgery?

Tim Jarman: Yes. I didn't really know what I was going to do, except that I was going to be rooted in the community. I was fortunate in making a friendship with a local teenager. We just knocked on doors, and said, 'What do *you* think we should do?' Most people said, 'Do something about the kids in the street.' The kids in the street were saying, 'It's boring, we need things to do,' and out of that came very extensive youth clubs, which for the first few years, in fact, met in my house.

Presenter: What did the youngsters do there?

Tim Jarman: Very ordinary things. You know, table-tennis, snooker, ball games. It was very crowded in my house, of course, and later on we found somewhere larger. But I think the essence was that it was their place. And there was an old greenhouse, just a lean-to against our house, and about 15 teenagers took that over as their den. And they came every night and met up with their friends there. So they were kept out of trouble, but they weren't having adults breathing down their neck. That's what counted, I think.

Presenter: After 10 years there, you moved away, but you went back to Northdown later, didn't you, to see how these teenagers had got on? What'd happened to them?

Tim Jarman: Well, I'd found a way of measuring the likelihood of their getting into trouble. When they first came to us, most of them were brought up in difficult circumstances, had problems at school, were in trouble with the police and so on. I set up a kind of risk table and worked out that 39% were at high risk of future unemployment, crime and unstable relationships. But the encouraging feature is that, now in their 30s, the majority of the youngsters have kept out of trouble, are in work and enjoy stable relationships. So the prediction was wrong, because something intervened to set things right. I'm not claiming our project was the whole factor, because clearly the availability of jobs, finding the right partner, making a good relationship were important, but all the 50 youngsters we interviewed said the project played a major part in their lives.

Presenter: So, is there a formula you think could be applied elsewhere?

Tim Jarman: Yes, the long-term nature of it, the combination of youth clubs and having social workers resident in the area who really get to know the young people. That's the core of it. The trouble is, our kind of project's no longer in the mainstream. Modern projects are very different, because the authorities are much keener on swift intervention, on targeting youngsters with problems, not treating them on a neighbourhood basis, a quick fix, in other words.

Presenter: I know you're critical of the initiatives some governments are adopting, giving people advice and counselling on how to be good parents.

[pause]

Now you'll hear Part Three again.

tone

[The recording is repeated.]

[pause]

That's the end of Part Three.

Now turn to Part Four.

[pause]

PART 4   *You will hear part of a conversation in which two neighbours, Mary and Frank, are discussing current developments in museums. For questions 23 to 28, decide whether the opinions are expressed by only one of the speakers, or whether the speakers agree. Write M for Mary, F for Frank, or B for both, where they agree.*

You now have thirty seconds in which to look at Part Four.

[pause]

tone

Mary: How was your weekend, Frank? Do anything nice?

Frank: Yes Mary, I did actually. We all went to the Science Museum.

Mary: I shouldn't think your children were very pleased at being taken round a lot of dusty exhibits.

Frank: Well, I know that's what people think, but lots of museums are really interesting these days.

Mary: Well, if you say so.

Frank: I know why you're sceptical. I remember when museums used to be just row after row of glass cabinets full of rocks or dead insects…

Mary: Aren't they still?

Frank: They're more interactive now. Kids can press buttons and touch things. It's really child-friendly.

Mary: But I thought museums were for learning.

Frank: Education doesn't have to be dull or stuffy, does it?

Mary: Not nowadays, at any rate. But why did you choose the Science Museum? Your children aren't very keen on science, are they?

Frank: Well, that's the point. I wanted to give them some encouragement, sort of sugar the pill. Actually, I found them a good booklet on the museum in the local library first and so they got interested in the exhibits before we went.

Mary: That must have been helpful.

Frank: Mmm, and it saves time when you actually visit, if you know what to focus on.

Mary: What about the cost? Museums charge quite a lot now, don't they? They were all free years ago, when I took my children.

Frank: Well, that's all a bit up in the air at the moment. Some places are still free, some just charge £1 for adults, and some charge quite a hefty sum.

Mary: I can see that charging is a thorny issue. But the collections in museums are national assets. So everyone should be able to have equal access to them, shouldn't they?

107

Frank:	There are *other* implications, like the theory that people are more likely to value something if they have to pay for it.
Mary:	Um, but let's look at public libraries. They're a national resource too.
Frank:	So?
Mary:	Well, it would be quite wrong if the local authorities started charging for access to them, claiming it would make children appreciate books more.
Frank:	But museums have to put on special events to attract more people, but books in a library don't change that much. And you know, some museums have an outreach system now, which I think is quite a positive move.
Mary:	Does that mean they take dinosaur skeletons and paintings round the country in a van!
Frank:	It would need a very large van for a dinosaur! No they send some of their collection, paintings etc. out to schools, libraries, community centres on temporary loan.
Mary:	Oh, I see. Well, it *is* a long way to the big museums from little towns like this. Hmm, I suppose that's quite a creative use of resources.
Frank:	Indeed.
Mary:	What was the building itself like? I saw a programme on TV about a new museum in the North, and the architecture was lovely, very light and airy.
Frank:	And I'm sure the sort of building really influences how you experience the contents.
Mary:	Well, perhaps I'd better see the Science Museum for myself.

[pause]

Now you'll hear Part Four again.

tone

[The recording is repeated.]

[pause]

That's the end of Part Four.

There will now be a pause of five minutes for you to copy your answers onto the separate answer sheet. Be sure to follow the numbering of all the questions. I'll remind you when there is one minute left, so that you're sure to finish in time.

[pause]

You have one more minute left.

[pause]

That's the end of the test. Please stop now. Your supervisor will now collect all the question papers and answer sheets.